MARTIN GARDNER'S FAVORITE
POETIC PARODIES

MARTIN GARDNER'S FAVORITE
POETIC PARODIES

─────────

EDITED BY
MARTIN GARDNER

 **Prometheus Books**
59 John Glenn Drive
Amherst, New York 14228-2197

Published 2001 by Prometheus Books

Inquiries should be addressed to
Prometheus Books
59 John Glenn Drive
Amherst, New York 14228–2197
VOICE: 716–691–0133, ext. 207
FAX: 716–564–2711
WWW.PROMETHEUSBOOKS.COM

05 04 03 02 01   5 4 3 2 1

Library of Congress Cataloging-in-Publication Data

Martin Gardner's favorite poetic parodies / edited by Martin Gardner.
        p. cm.
    ISBN 1–57392–925–5 (alk. paper)
    1. Parodies. 2. English poetry. 3. American poetry. I. Title: Poetic Parodies. II. Gardner, Martin, 1914–

PR1195.P27 M37 2001
821.008—dc21   2001048130

Printed in Canada on acid-free paper

To Frank (on a roll) Jacobs

Whose Parodies top them all

O bards of rhyme and metre free,
My gratitude goes out to ye
For all your deathless lines—ahem!
Let's see, now. . . . What *is* one of them?

From *To a Vers Librist*,
by F. P. Adams in *Something Else Again*

CONTENTS

    John Greenleaf Whittier   189

43. The Burial of Sir John Moore
    Charles Wolfe   207

44. The Old Oaken Bucket
    Samuel Woodworth   211

45. Mary's Little Lamb
    Sarah Hale   229

46. Jabberwocky
    Lewis Carroll   231

47. A Visit From St. Nicholas
    Clement Clarke Moore   235

48. The Purple Cow
    Gelett Burgess   239

    Appendix: If Famous Poets Had Different Occupations
    Frank Jacobs   241

INTRODUCTION

There are two kinds of verse parodies: parodies of style only, usually not funny, and comic parodies of well known poems. Almost all anthologies of parodies are of the first type, such as Louis Untermeyer's *Collected Parodies* (1919) and Dwight Macdonald's *Parodies* (1960). So many burlesques were written in the manner of Walt Whitman that Henry Saunders edited an entire book of them: *Parodies of Walt Whitman* (1922).

Several book length parodies of Omar's *Rubaiyat* have been published, notably *The Rubaiyat of Omar Cayenne* (1904), by Gelett Burgess, and *The Rubaiyat of a Persian Kitten* (1904), by Oliver Herford. A few writers have produced collections of parodies all written by themselves, but they are mainly parodies of style. A recent exception is Frank Jacobs's *Pitiless Parodies and Other Outrageous Verse* (1994). I consider Jacobs the finest writer in English of hilarious parodies of famous poems, most of them first published in *Mad* magazine.

Unlike anthologies of parodies of style, the book you hold is a collection of an entirely different sort. It contains only funny parodies of poems so famous that most readers, without being told, will at once recognize the poem being parodied.

As far as I know, Carolyn Wells's *A Parody Anthology* (1919) was the first collection mainly of comic parodies of specific poems. A long section of such parodies can also be found in her *Book of Humorous Verse* (1920). A more recent collection of a similar sort is Myra Cohn Livingston's *Speak Roughly to Your Little Boy* (1971). The title is the first line of Lewis Carroll's parody of *Speak Gently*, by David Bates, a popular sentimental poem of the time. (For Carroll's other parodies of verse in his two *Alice* books, see the new 2000 edition of my *Annotated Alice*.)

It goes without saying that a comic parody is most effective when the reader is familiar with all the lines of the poem being spoofed. In this collection, I have omitted all parodies of poems now so completely forgotten that most of their humor is lost on today's readers. As an aid to those who may know the original verse but cannot recall all its lines, I have provided here the poems that are parodied. These originals can also be found in my two Dover collections, *Best Remembered Poems* (1992) and *Famous Poems From Bygone Days* (1995), along with introductions to each poem that tell something about the author and the poem's history.

The two most parodied poems in English are Ernest Thayer's *Casey at the Bat* and Clement Moore's *Visit From St. Nicholas*. Many of their burlesques are gathered in my *Annotated Casey at the Bat*, currently available as a Dover 1995 reprint, and my *Annotated Night Before Christmas* (1991), now out of print.

Next to those two poems, the two most parodied English poems are surely Edgar Allan Poe's *The Raven* and Samuel Woodworth's *The Old Oaken Bucket*. An entire book could easily be confined to take-offs of each poem. I have selected here only the *Raven* and the *Bucket* spoofs that I consider the best.

It is hard now to comprehend the enormous popularity *The Old Oaken Bucket* once had. It was set to music. Copies were framed and hung in living rooms. Stanzas were embroidered and framed. Hundreds of illustrations accompanied the poem's reprintings in newspapers and magazines. Handsome engravings, many in full color, were sold, including two by Currier and Ives.

Today, Woodworth's *Oaken Bucket* is almost forgotten, and considered sentimental doggerel by critics. Yet, like most popular verse, the poem is well crafted, and at least has a melodic structure that distinguishes it from the dull prose that now disguises itself as poetry. The fact that the poem was so often spoofed is a double tribute—to the extent it was so universally loved, and to the extent that so many critics thought it worthless.

Tracking down parodies of famous poems is not easy because so many are buried in old newspapers and periodicals where they are difficult to unearth. I recall, as a boy, reading a funny poem titled *Out Where the Vest Begins*, but I haven't the slightest notion of where or when I saw it. If such poems are listed in periodical guides or verse indexes it is often impossible to recognize them from their titles. Parodies of Poe's *Raven* were plentiful in American newspapers and magazines in the years soon after the poem was first printed in a newspaper. I have made no effort to run these down because it would require tedious weeks of rolling microfilm in the Library of Congress.

Only five parodies by Frank Jacobs (aside from those in the appendix) are in this collection. I originally hoped to include a dozen more, all from *Mad* magazine, but the publisher of *Mad* demanded a thousand dollars in advance against 2 percent of the book's royalties! The five included here are owned by Jacobs who has generously allowed me to reprint them at no charge. The twelve owned by *Mad* can all be found in Jacobs's Dover paperback, *Pitiless Parodies and Other Outrageous Verse*.

I would like to thank philosopher Peter Heath and correspondent Julia Oxreider for calling my attention to poems I otherwise would have missed, and to friend Russell Barnhart for yeoman research at the New York Public Library. And I owe special debts to Frank Jacobs and Armand T. Ringer for allowing me to include so many of their poems.

Martin Gardner

1.

MEMORY

By Thomas Bailey Aldrich

My mind lets go a thousand things,
Like dates of wars and deaths of kings,
And yet recalls the very hour—
'T was noon by yonder village tower,
And on the last blue noon in May
The wind came briskly up this way,
Crisping the brook beside the road;
Then, pausing here, set down its load
Of pine-scents, and shook listlessly
Two petals from that wild-rose tree.

MEMORY

By Armand T. Ringer

My mind lets go a thousand things,
Like dates of wars and deaths of kings,
And yet recalls the very hour—
'Twas noon by yonder village tower.
And on the last blue moon in May
A cow came briskly up the way,
Along the brook beside the road;
Then, pausing here, set down its load
Of pungent scents, then listlessly
Two sparrows flew down from a tree.

2.

ROCK ME TO SLEEP

By Elizabeth Akers Allen

Backward, turn backward, O Time, in your flight,
Make me a child again just for to-night!
Mother, come back from the echoless shore,
Take me again to your heart as of yore;
Kiss from my forehead the furrows of care,
Smooth the few silver threads out of my hair;
Over my slumbers your loving watch keep—
Rock me to sleep, mother—rock me to sleep!

Backward, flow backward, O tide of the years!
I am so weary of toil and of tears—
Toil without recompense, tears all in vain—
Take them and give me my childhood again!
I have grown weary of dust and decay,
Weary of flinging my soul-wealth away,
Weary of sowing for others to reap—
Rock me to sleep, mother—rock me to sleep!

Tired of the hollow, the base, the untrue,
Mother, O mother, my heart calls for you!
Many a summer the grass has grown green,
Blossomed and faded, our faces between;
Yet, with strong yearning and passionate pain,
Long I to-night for your presence again;
Come from the silence so long and so deep—
Rock me to sleep, mother—rock me to sleep!

19

Over my heart in the days that are flown,
No love like mother-love ever has shone;
No other worship abides and endures,
Faithful, unselfish, and patient, like yours;
None like a mother can charm away pain
From the sick soul and the world-weary brain;
Slumber's soft calms o'er my heavy lids creep—
Rock me to sleep, mother—rock me to sleep!

Come, let your brown hair, just lighted with gold,
Fall on your shoulders again as of old;
Let it drop over my forehead to-night,
Shading my faint eyes away from the light;
For with its sunny-edged shadows once more,
Haply will throng the sweet visions of yore;
Lovingly, softly, its bright billows sweep—
Rock me to sleep, mother—rock me to sleep!

Mother, dear mother, the years have been long
Since I last listened your lullaby song;
Sing, then, and unto my soul it shall seem
Womanhood's years have been only a dream.
Clasped to your heart in a loving embrace,
With your light lashes just sweeping my face,
Never hereafter to wake or to weep—
Rock me to sleep, mother—rock me to sleep!

A MIDSUMMER PRAYER

**By Walt Mason, in the Virginia Gazette
(September 2, 1915)**

Backward, turn backward, oh, time in thy flight.
Give us some snow again, just for tonight!
Give us a blast from the boreal shore
Shaking the windows and rattling the door!
I am so weary of weather that fries,
I am so weary of swatting the flies,
Weary of swearing in truculent tones,
Weary of blowing my ill-gotten bones
Down at the drug store for fizzstuff in cans,
Weary of sitting by rickety fans.
Auntie, come back from the shadowy shore.
Dope me for chilblains again, as of yore;
Talk about gum-drops and other things nice—
Put me on ice, auntie, put me on ice!

Backward, turn backward, oh, tide of the years!
Give us some frost-bitten fingers and ears!
Give us a blizzard, with all kinds of sleet,
Give us a stem-winding storm and repeat!
Auntie, who loved me in time long ago,
Bring to your dear little Willie some snow!
I have been baking until I'm well done;
I have been sizzling away in the sun;
I have been cooked in the old-fashioned style;
I have been fricasseed, mile after mile;
I am now scrambled and ready to serve;
I am reduced to a bundle of nerve.
Come, then, and save me—one more will suffice—
Put me on ice, auntie, put me on ice!

3.

THE NIGHT HAS A THOUSAND EYES

By Francis William Bourdillon

The night has a thousand eyes,
    And the day but one;
Yet the light of the bright world dies
    With the dying sun.

The mind has a thousand eyes,
    And the heart but one;
Yet the light of a whole life dies
    When love is done.

THE CLOSET HAS A HUNDRED TIES

By Armand T. Ringer

My father had a hundred ties
    And I but one.
"Will you give me three?" I asked.
    He smiled and said, "My son,
You may take three provided you
    Take more than eighty-one."

4.

THE GOLF LINKS

By Sarah Norcliffe Cleghorn

The golf links lie so near the mill
    That almost every day
The laboring children can look out
    And see the men at play.

THE WEB LINKS

By Armand T. Ringer

The web links sprout inside our home,
    And almost every day
When I come home from work I find
    My kids at online play.

5.

This ballad is too long to quote. Here are its opening stanzas:

THE ANCIENT MARINER

By Samuel Taylor Coleridge

It is an ancient mariner,
And he stoppeth one of three.
"By thy long gray beard and glittering eye,
Now wherefore stopp'st thou me?

The bridegroom's doors are opened wide,
And I am next of kin;
The guests are met, the feast is set,—
May'st hear the merry din."

He holds him with his skinny hand:
"There was a ship," quoth he.
"Hold off! unhand me, graybeard loon!"—
Eftsoons his hand dropt he.

He holds him with his glittering eye,—
The wedding-guest stood still;
He listens like a three years' child;
The mariner hath his will.

The wedding-guest sat on a stone,—
He cannot choose but hear;

And thus spake on that ancient man,
The bright-eyed mariner:

"The ship was cheered, the harbor cleared;
Merrily did we drop
Below the kirk, below the hill,
Below the lighthouse top.

The sun came up upon the left,
Out of the sea came he;
And he shone bright, and on the right
Went down into the sea.

SALTY BORE

By William Cole

It was an ancient mariner,
And he stoppeth one of three;
The two unstoppeth carrieth on—
The stoppeth cried, "Why me?"

THE ANCIENT MARINER

By Anonymous

It is an Ancient Mariner,
And he stoppeth one of three—
In fact he coolly took my arm—
"There was a ship," quoth he.

"Bother your ships!" said I, "is this
The time a yarn to spin?
This is a wedding, don't you see,
And I am next of kin.

The wedding breakfast has begun,
We're hungry as can be—
Hold off! Unhand me, longshore man!"
With that his hand dropt he.

But there was something in his eye,
That made me sick and ill,
Yet forced to listen to his yarn—
The Mariner'd had his will.

While Tom and Harry went their way
I sat upon a stone—
So queer on Fanny's wedding day
Me sitting there alone!

Then he began, that Mariner,
To rove from pole to pole,
In one long-winded, lengthened-out,
Eternal rigmarole,

About a ship in which he'd sailed,
Though whither, goodness knows,
Where "ice will split with a thunder-fit,"
And every day it snows.

And then about a precious bird
Of some sort or another,
That—was such nonsense ever heard?—
Used to control the weather!

Now, at this bird the Mariner
Resolved to have a shy,
And laid it low with his cross-bow—
And then the larks! My eye!

For loss of that uncommon fowl,
They couldn't get a breeze;
And there they stuck, all out of luck,
And rotted on the seas.

The crew all died, or seemed to die,
And he was left alone
With that queer bird. You never heard
What games were carried on!

At last one day he stood and watched
The fishes in the sea,
And said, "I'm blest!" and so the ship
Was from the spell set free.

And it began to rain and blow,
And as it rained and blew,
The dead got up and worked the ship—
That was a likely crew!

However, somehow he escaped,
And got again to land,
But mad as any hatter, say,
From Cornhill to the Strand.

For he believes that certain folks
Are singled out by fate,
To whom this cock-and-bull affair
Of his he must relate.

Describing all the incidents,
And painting all the scenes,
As sailors will do in the tales
They tell to the Marines.

Confound the Ancient Mariner!
I knew I should be late;
And so it was; the wedding guests
Had all declined to wait.

Another had my place, and gave
My toast; and sister Fan
Said "'Twas a shame. What could you want
With that seafaring man?"

I felt like one that had been stunned
Through all this wrong and scorn;
A sadder and a later man
I rose the morrow morn.

THE ANCIENT SHORTSTOP

By Armand T. Ringer

He was an ancient shortstop
Who stoppeth one of three.
With his long gray beard and one glass eye,
No wonder he couldn't see!

6.

To a Fat Lady Seen From the Train

By Frances Cornford

O why do you walk through the fields in gloves,
    Missing so much and so much?
O fat white woman whom nobody loves,
Why do you walk through the fields in gloves,
When the grass is soft as the breast of doves
    And shivering-sweet to the touch?
O why do you walk through the fields in gloves,
    Missing so much and so much?

The Fat Lady Speaks

By G. K. Chesterton

Why do you rush through the field in trains,
Guessing so much and so much.
Why do you flash through the flowery meads,
Fat-head poet that nobody reads;
And why do you know such a frightful lot
About people in gloves as such?

And how the devil can you be sure,
Guessing so much and so much,
How do you know but what someone who loves
Always to see me in nice white gloves

33

At the end of the field you are rushing by,
Is waiting for his Old Dutch?

THE LADY EXPLAINS

By Armand T. Ringer

O why do you walk through the fields in gloves
    On past the church and the school?
O beautiful woman whom everyone loves,
Why do you walk through the fields in gloves,
When the grass is soft as the breast of doves,
    And breezes blow sweet and cool?
O why do you walk through the fields in gloves?
    "To avoid poison ivy, you fool!"

7.

BEN BOLT

By Thomas Dunn English

Don't you remember sweet Alice, Ben Bolt,—
    Sweet Alice whose hair was so brown,
Who wept with delight when you gave her a smile,
    And trembled with fear at your frown?

In the old churchyard in the valley, Ben Bolt,
    In a corner obscure and alone,
They have fitted a slab of the granite so gray,
    And Alice lies under the stone.

Under the hickory tree, Ben Bolt,
    Which stood at the foot of the hill,
Together we've lain in the noonday shade,
    And listened to Appleton's mill.

The mill-wheel has fallen to pieces, Ben Bolt,
    The rafters have tumbled in,
And a quiet which crawls round the walls as you gaze
    Has followed the olden din.

Do you mind of the cabin of logs, Ben Bolt,
    At the edge of the pathless wood,
And the button-ball tree with its motley limbs,
    Which nigh by the doorstep stood?

35

The cabin to ruin has gone, Ben Bolt,
　　The tree you would seek for in vain;
And where once the lords of the forest waved,
　　Are grass and the golden grain.

And don't you remember the school, Ben Bolt,
　　With the master so cruel and grim,
And the shaded nook in the running brook
　　Where the children went to swim?

Grass grows on the master's grave, Ben Bolt,
　　The spring of the brook is dry,
And of all the boys who were schoolmates then
　　There are only you and I.

There is change in the things I loved, Ben Bolt,
　　They have changed from the old to the new;
But I feel in the depths of my spirit the truth,
　　There never was change in you.

Twelvemonths twenty have passed, Ben Bolt,
　　Since first we were friends—yet I hail
Your presence a blessing, your friendship a truth,
　　Ben Bolt of the salt-sea gale!

JOE JONES

By Anonymous

Don't you remember lame Sally, Joe Jones—
　　Lame Sally, whose nose was so brown?
Who looked like a clam if you gave her a smile,
　　And went into fits at your frown?
In the old goose-pond in the orchard, Joe Jones,
　　Where the goslings are learning to swim,

Lame Sally went fishing one wet, windy day,
    And there by mistake tumbled in.

Under old Sim's brush fence, Joe Jones,
    That winds at the foot of the hill,
Together we've seen the old camel go round,
    Grinding cider at Appleton's mill;
The mill-wheel is oven-wood now, Joe Jones,
    The rafters fell on to a cow,
And the weasels and rats, that crawl round as you gaze,
    Are the lords of the cider-mill now.

Do you remember the pig-pen of logs, Joe Jones,
    Which stood on the path to the barn?
And the shirt button trees, where they grew on the boughs,
    Which we sewed on our jackets with yarn?
The pig-pen has gone to decay, Joe Jones,
    And the lightning the tree overcome;
And down where the onions and carrots once grew,
    Grow thistles as big as your thumb.

Don't you remember the school, Joe Jones?
    And the master who wore the old wig?
And the nice shady nook by the crook of the brook,
    Where we played with Aunt Catharine's pig?
Mice live in the master's wig, Joe Jones,
    The brook with the crook is now dry,
And the boys and the girls that were playmates then,
    Have grown up ever so high.

There's a change in the things I love, Joe Jones,
    They have changed from the good to the bad—
And I feel in my stomach, to tell you the truth,
    I'd like to go home to my dad.
Twelve times twelve months have passed, Joe Jones,
    Since I knocked off your nose with a rail;

And yet I believe I'm your own true friend,
  Joe Jones of the Hurricane Gale!

THE NEW ALICE

By Franklin P. Adams,
from **So Then!** *(Doubleday Page, 1923)*

Oh, have you observed your sweet Alice, Ben Bolt—
  Sweet Alice with hair now so titian?
She screams with delight when you play her some jazz,
  And to toddle all night's her ambition.
She swims and she rides and she motors, Ben Bolt;
  She smokes, and she wallops the ball;
And to-night when I asked her about you, Ben Bolt,
  Why, she didn't remember you at all—
When I asked her to-night how about you, Ben Bolt,
  Why, she failed to recall you at all.

8.

THE HOUSE BY THE SIDE OF THE ROAD

By Sam Walter Foss

> *"He was a friend to man, and he lived*
> *In a house by the side of the road." —Homer.*

There are hermit souls that live withdrawn
    In the place of their self-content;
There are souls like stars, that dwell apart,
    In a fellowless firmament;
There are pioneer souls that blaze their paths
    Where highways never ran—
But let me live by the side of the road
    And be a friend to man.

Let me live in a house by the side of the road,
    Where the race of men go by—
The men who are good and the men who are bad,
    As good and as bad as I.
I would not sit in the scorner's seat,
    Or hurl the cynic's ban—
Let me live in a house by the side of the road
    And be a friend to man.

I see from my house by the side of the road,
    By the side of the highway of life,
The men who press with the ardor of hope,
    The men who are faint with the strife.

They beckon you forth to wide spaces,
To a lifted and far-shining goal,
To a new federation of races
And a fatherland fit for the soul
                            Sam Walter Foss

Sam Walter Foss

But I turn not away from their smiles nor their tears,
    Both parts of an infinite plan—
Let me live in a house by the side of the road
    And be a friend to man.

I know there are brook-gladdened meadows ahead
    And mountains of wearisome height;
That the road passes on through the long afternoon
    And stretches away to the night.
But still I rejoice when the travelers rejoice,
    And weep with the strangers that moan,
Nor live in my house by the side of the road
    Like a man who dwells alone.

Let me live in my house by the side of the road—
    It's here the race of men go by.
They are good, they are bad, they are weak, they are strong,
    Wise, foolish—so am I;
Then why should I sit in the scorner's seat,
    Or hurl the cynic's ban?
Let me live in my house by the side of the road
    And be a friend to man.

A HOUSE FAR AWAY FROM THE ROAD

By Armand T. Ringer

I'm a hermit soul who lives withdrawn
In the peace of my self-content,
Far from the fumes of trailers and trucks
That pollute the firmament.
There are souls who love to clog the paths
Where once the rabbits ran.
Let me live in my house far away from the road.
As far from the road as I can.

Let me live in a house far away from the road
Where the garbage trucks roar by.
Some drivers are good, some drivers are bad,
As good and as bad as I.
Why should I envy the motorist's seat
Tailgated by truck or van?
Let me live in a house far away from the road,
Far from the highways of man.

I'll stay in my home far away from the roads,
Away from the thruways of life,
Where the drivers too high on the booze or on dope
Are the drivers who faint from the strife.
I am eager to turn from their snarls and their snorts
To live by a happier plan
In a house far away from the rage of the road,
And try to write verses that scan.

I much prefer brook-gladdened meadows and trees,
And mountains of marvelous height,
To the gigantic signs for tobacco and beer,
And exhausts that hang on through the night,
I cannot rejoice when the truckers rejoice
Or weep with the drivers who moan.
I live in my house far away from the road
Like a hermit who dwells alone.

Let me live far away from the side of the road
Where traffic rolls endlessly by.
Some drivers are weak, some others are strong,
Wise, foolish — so am I.
Why should I envy the motorist's seat
At the wheel of a truck or a van?
Let me live in my house far away from the road,
As far as I possibly can.

9.

THE ROAD NOT TAKEN

By Robert Frost

Two roads diverged in a yellow wood,
And sorry I could not travel both
And be one traveler, long I stood
And looked down one as far as I could
To where it bent in the undergrowth;

Then took the other, as just as fair,
And having perhaps the better claim,
Because it was grassy and wanted wear;
Though as for that the passing there
Had worn them really about the same,

And both that morning equally lay
In leaves no step had trodden black.
Oh, I kept the first for another day!
Yet knowing how way leads on to way,
I doubted if I should ever come back.

I shall be telling this with a sigh
Somewhere ages and ages hence:
Two roads diverged in a wood, and I—
I took the one less traveled by,
And that has made all the difference.

THE ROAD I TOOK

By Armand T. Ringer

Two roads diverged in Kansas City.
Sorry I couldn't travel each,
And be one traveler. What a pity!
I looked down one—the path was gritty
As far as my bloodshot eyes could reach.

I shall be telling this with a sigh,
Mingled with all my hopes and fears:
Two roads diverged in the city, and I—
I took the one less traveled by.
I'll be out of prison in fifteen years.

10.

STOPPING BY WOODS ON A SNOWY EVENING

By Robert Frost

Whose woods these are I think I know.
His house is in the village though;
He will not see me stopping here
To watch his woods fill up with snow.

My little horse must think it queer
To stop without a farmhouse near
Between the woods and frozen lake
The darkest evening of the year.

He gives his harness bells a shake
To ask if there is some mistake.
The only other sound's the sweep
Of easy wind and downy flake.

The woods are lovely, dark and deep.
But I have promises to keep,
And miles to go before I sleep,
And miles to go before I sleep.

STOPPING BY WOODS TO FIND MY GOLF BALL

By James Brooks

Which woods these are I damn well know.
I've been here twenty times or so.
My partners snicker when I'm here;
Now where the hell did that ball go?

Squirrels and birds must think it queer
To see me with no fairway near.
Between my ball and closest rough
Lie endless trees; I shed a tear.

I take a swing, I huff and puff.
"I'll hit this thing; it's not that tough!"
And then I hear another knock
Of ball on trunk; "I've had enough!"

The squirrels are running, the birds have flit,
But I have recovery shots to hit,
And miles to go before I putt,
And miles to go before I putt.

11.

FIRE AND ICE

By Robert Frost

Some say the world will end in fire,
Some say in ice.
From what I've tasted of desire
I hold with those who favor fire.
But if it had to perish twice,
I think I know enough of hate
To say that for destruction ice
Is also great
And would suffice.

WARM OR COLD

By Armand T. Ringer

Some say that booze is best when warm.
Some say on ice.
I hold with those who favor warm,
But if I had to drink it twice
I think I know enough of late
To say that for one's pleasure ice
Is also great
And would suffice

12.

It Couldn't Be Done

By Eddie Guest

Somebody said that it couldn't be done,
    But he with a chuckle replied
That "maybe it couldn't," but he would be one

    Who wouldn't say so till he'd tried.
So he buckled right in with the trace of a grin
    On his face. If he worried he hid it.
He started to sing as he tackled the thing
    That couldn't be done, and he did it.

Somebody scoffed: "Oh, you'll never do that;
    At least no one ever has done it;"
But he took off his coat and he took off his hat,
    And the first thing we knew he'd begun it.
With a lift of his chin and a bit of a grin,
    Without any doubting or quiddit,
He started to sing as he tackled the thing
    That couldn't be done, and he did it.

There are thousands to tell you it cannot be done,
    There are thousands to prophesy failure;
There are thousands to point out to you one by one,
    The dangers that wait to assail you.
But just buckle in with a bit of a grin,
    Just take off your coat and go to it;

Just start in to sing as you tackle the thing
   That "cannot be done," and you'll do it.

When It Can't Be Done

By Armand T. Ringer

Somebody said that it couldn't be done,
   But he with a chuckle replied
That "maybe it couldn't," but he would be one
   Who wouldn't say so till he'd tried.
So he buckled right in with the trace of a grin
   If he worried, no friend of his knew it.
He started to sing as he tackled the thing,
   And sure 'nuff, the poor chap couldn't do it.

Somebody scoffed: "Oh, you'll never do that;
   At least no one ever has done it;"
But he took off his coat and he took off his hat,
   And the first thing we knew he'd begun it.
With a lift of his chin and a bit of a grin,
   In a couple of hours he blew it.
He started to sing as he tackled the thing.
   By golly! He just couldn't do it!

There are thousands to tell you it cannot be done,
   There are thousands to prophesy failure;
There are thousands to point out to you one by one,
   The dangers that wait to assail you.
But just buckle in with a bit of a grin,
   Just take off your coat and go to it.
Just start in to sing as you tackle the thing,
   'Til it dawns on you, no one can do it!

13.

I Remember, I Remember

By Thomas Hood

I remember, I remember,
    The house where I was born,
The little window where the sun
    Came peeping in at morn:
He never came a wink too soon,
    Nor brought too long a day;
But now, I often wish the night
    Had borne my breath away.

I remember, I remember,
    The roses, red and white;
The violets and the lily-cups,
    Those flowers made of light!
The lilacs where the robin built,
    And where my brother set
The laburnum on his birthday,—
    The tree is living yet!

I remember, I remember,
    Where I was used to swing;
And thought the air must rush as fresh
    To swallows on the wing:
My spirit flew in feathers then,
    That is so heavy now,
And summer pools could hardly cool
    The fever on my brow!

I remember, I remember,
   The fir trees dark and high;
I used to think their slender tops
   Were close against the sky:

It was a childish ignorance,
   But now 'tis little joy
To know I'm farther off from heaven
   Than when I was a boy.

I REMEMBER

By Franklin P. Adams, in Something Else Again (1920)

I remember, I remember
The house where I was born;
The rent was thirty-two a month,
Which made my father mourn.
He said he could remember when
His father paid the rent;
And when a man's expenses did
Not take his every cent.

I remember, I remember—
My mother telling my cousin
That eggs had gone to twenty-six
Or seven cents a dozen;
And how she told my father that
She didn't like to speak
Of things like that, but Bridget now
Demanded four a week.

I remember, I remember—
And with a mirthless laugh—
My weekly board at college took

A jump to three and a half.
I bought an eighteen-dollar suit,
And father told me, "Sonny,
I'll pay the bill this time, but,
Oh, I am not made of money!"

I remember, I remember,
When I was young and brave
And I declared, "Well, Birdie, we
Shall now begin to save."
It was a childish ignorance,
But now 'tis little joy
To know I'm farther off from wealth
Than when I was a boy.

PAST AND PRESENT

By Carolyn Wells

I remember, I remember
    The flat where I was born:
The little air-shaft where the sun
    Could not peep through at morn;
The stuffy rooms and narrow halls
    Unlit by Heaven's ray;
The seven winding flights of stairs
    That took my breath away

I remember, I remember
    The sickly daffodils
That bloomed in old tomato-cans
    Upon the window-sills;
The cupboard where the cake was kept,
    And where my brother set
A patent trap to catch a mouse,—
    That mouse is living yet!

I remember, I remember
    The sounds I used to know:
The organ on the floor above,
    The violin below;
The cats upon the fire-escape,
    The steam-heat in the wall;
The chorus-girl a-singing in—
    The flat across the hall.

I remember, I remember
    The scuttle dark and high
Through which I often used to climb
    To get a glimpse of sky.
I live in first-floor chambers now,
    With nothing to annoy,
But still I in farther off from Heaven
    Than when I was a boy.

14.

Abou Ben Adhem

By Leigh Hunt

Abou Ben Adhem (may his tribe increase!)
Awoke one night from a deep dream of peace,
And saw, within the moonlight in his room,
Making it rich, and like a lily in bloom,
An angel writing in a book of gold:—
Exceeding peace had made Ben Adhem bold,
And to the presence in the room he said,
    "What writest thou?"—The vision rais'd its head,
And with a look made of all sweet accord,
Answer'd, "The names of those who love the Lord."
    "And is mine one?" asked Abou. "Nay, not so,"
Replied the angel. Abou spoke more low,
But cheerly still; and said, "I pray thee, then,
Write me as one that loves his fellow men."
    The angel wrote, and vanish'd. The next night
It came again with a great wakening light,
And show'd the names whom love of God had blest,
And lo! Ben Adhem's name led all the rest.

ABOU BEN BUTLER*

By John Paul, pseudonym of Charles Henry Webb

Abou, Ben Butler (may his tribe be less!)
Awoke one night from a deep bottledness,
And saw, by the rich radiance of the moon,
Which shone and shimmered like a silver spoon,
A stranger writing on a golden slate
(Exceeding store had Ben of spoons and plate),
And to the stranger in his tent he said:
    "Your little game?" The stranger turned his head,
And, with a look made all of innocence,
Replied: "I write the name of Presidents."
    "And is mine one?" "Not if this court doth know
Itself," replied the stranger. Ben said, "Oh!"
And "Ah!" but spoke again: "Just name your price
To write me up as one that may be Vice."
    The stranger up and vanished. The next night
He came again, and showed a wondrous sight
Of names that haply yet might fill the chair—
But, lo, I the name of Butler was not there!

*Benjamin Franklin Butler (1818–1893) was an American Army general and politician
who wanted to be president.

15.

JENNY KISS'D ME

By Leigh Hunt

Jenny kiss'd me when we met,
    Jumping from the chair she sat in;
Time, you thief, who love to get
    Sweets into your list, put that in!
Say I'm weary, say I'm sad,
    Say that health and wealth have miss'd me,
Say I'm growing old, but add,
    Jenny kiss'd me.

SUCH STUFF AS DREAMS

By Franklin P. Adams, in **Something Else Again** *(1920)*

Jenny kiss'd me in a dream;
    So did Elsie, Lucy, Cora,
Bessie, Gwendolyn, Eupheme,
    Alice, Adelaide, and Dora.
Say of honour I'm devoid,
    Say monogamy has miss'd me,
But don't say to Dr. Freud
    Jenny kiss'd me.

JENNY KISSED ME

By Paul Dehn

Jenny kiss'd me when we met,
    Jumping from the chair she sat in;
Time, you thief, who love to get
    Sweets into your list, put that in!
Say I'm weary, say I'm old,
    Say that health and wealth have miss'd me,
Say I've had a filthy cold
    Since Jenny kiss'd me.

JENNY MERELY KISSED ME

By Bruce E. Newling

Jenny kissed me when we met.
    She, adorned in silk and satin,
Told me, "That is all you get;
    And as you leave, don't let the cat in."
Retrospection makes me glad:
    Dread disease perhaps thus missed me.
God knows what I might have had
    Had Jenny more than merely kissed me.

16

ODE TO A NIGHTINGALE

By John Keats

I

My heart aches, and a drowsy numbness pains
    My sense, as though of hemlock I had drunk,
Or emptied some dull opiate to the drains
    One minute past, and Lethe-wards had sunk:
'Tis not through envy of thy happy lot,
    But being too happy in thine happiness,—
        That thou, light-winged Dryad of the trees,
            In some melodious plot
Of beechen green, and shadows numberless,
    Singest of summer in full-throated ease.

II

O, for a draught of vintage! that hath been
    Cool'd a long age in the deep-delved earth,
Tasting of Flora and the country green,
    Dance, and Provençal song, and sunburnt mirth!
O for a beaker full of the warm South,
    Full of the true, the blushful Hippocrene,
        With beaded bubbles winking at the brim,
            And purple-stained mouth;
That I might drink, and leave the world unseen,
    And with thee fade away into the forest dim:

III

Fade far away, dissolve, and quite forget
    What thou among the leaves hast never known,
The weariness, the fever, and the fret
    Here, where men sit and hear each other groan;
Where palsy shakes a few, sad, last gray hairs,
    Where youth grows pale, and spectre-thin, and dies;
        Where but to think is to be full of sorrow
        And leaden-eyed despairs,
Where Beauty cannot keep her lustrous eyes,
    Or new Love pine at them beyond to-morrow.

IV

Away! away! for I will fly to thee,
    Not charioted by Bacchus and his pards,
But on the viewless wings of Poesy,
    Though the dull brain perplexes and retards:
Already with thee! tender is the night,
    And haply the Queen-Moon is on her throne,
        Cluster'd around by all her starry Fays;
            But here there is no light,
    Save what from heaven is with the breezes blown
        Through verdurous glooms and winding mossy ways.

V

I cannot see what flowers are at my feet,
    Nor what soft incense hangs upon the boughs,
But, in embalmed darkness, guess each sweet
    Wherewith the seasonable month endows
The grass, the thicket, and the fruit-tree wild;
    White hawthorn, and the pastoral eglantine;
        Fast fading violets cover'd up in leaves;
            And mid-May's eldest child,

The coming musk-rose, full of dewy wine,
　　The murmurous haunts of flies on summer eves.

VI

Darkling I listen; and, for many a time
　　I have been half in love with easeful Death,
Call'd him soft names in many a mused rhyme,
　　To take into the air my quiet breath;
Now more than ever seems it rich to die,
　　To cease upon the midnight with no pain,
　　　　While thou art pouring forth thy soul abroad
　　　　　　In such an ecstasy!
　　Still wouldst thou sing, and I have ears in vain
　　　　To thy high requiem become a sod.

VII

Thou wast not born for death, immortal Bird!
　　No hungry generations tread thee down;
The voice I hear this passing night was heard
　　In ancient days by emperor and clown:
Perhaps the self-same song that found a path
　　Through the sad heart of Ruth, when, sick for home,
　　　　She stood in tears amid the alien corn;
　　　　　　The same that oft-times hath
　　Charm'd magic casements, opening on the foam
　　　　Of perilous seas, in faery lands forlorn.

VIII

Forlorn! the very word is like a bell
　　To toll me back from thee to my sole self!
Adieu! the fancy cannot cheat so well
　　As she is fam'd to do, deceiving elf.
Adieu! adieu! thy plaintive anthem fades

Past the near meadows, over the still stream,
    Up the hill-side; and now 'tis buried deep
      In the next valley-glades:
Was it a vision, or a waking dream?
    Fled is that music:—Do I wake or sleep?

ODE TO A JAR OF PICKLES

By Bayward Taylor

I

A sweet, acidulous, down-reaching thrill
    Pervades my sense. I seem to see or hear
The lushy garden-grounds of Greenwich Hill
    In autumn, where the crispy leaves are sere;
And odors haunt me of remotest spice
    From the Levant or musky-aired Cathay,
Or from the saffron-fields of Jericho,
      Where everything is nice.
    The more I sniff, the more I swoon away,
And what else mortal palate craves, forego.

II

Odors unsmelled are keen, but those I smell
    Are keener; wherefore let me sniff again!
Enticing walnuts, I have known ye well
    In youth, when pickles were a passing pain;
Unwitting youth, that craves the candy stem,
    And sugar plums to olives doth prefer,
And even licks the pots of marmalade
      When sweetness clings to them.
    But now I dream of ambergris and myrrh,
Tasting these walnuts in the poplar shade.

III

Lo! hoarded coolness in the heart of noon,
    Plucked with its dew, the cucumber is here,
As to the Dryad's parching lips a boon,
    And crescent bean-pods, unto Bacchus dear;
And, last of all, the pepper's pungent globe,
    The scarlet dwelling of the sylph of fire,
Provoking purple draughts; and, surfeited,
        I cast my trailing robe
    O'er my pale feet, touch up my tuneless lyre,
And twist the Delphic wreath to suit my head.

IV

Here shall my tongue in otherwise be soured
    Than fretful men's in parched and palsied days;
And, by the mid-May's dusky leaves embowered,
    Forget the fruitful blame, the scanty praise.
No sweets to them who sweet themselves were born,
    Whose natures ooze with lucent saccharine;
Who, with sad repetition soothly cloyed,
        The lemon-tinted morn
    Enjoy, and find acetic twilight fine.
Wake I, or sleep? The pickle-jar is void.

17.

TREES

By Joyce Kilmer

I think that I shall never see
A poem lovely as a tree.

A tree whose hungry mouth is prest
Against the earth's sweet flowing breast;

A tree that looks at God all day,
And lifts her leafy arms to pray;

A tree that may in Summer wear
A nest of robins in her hair;

Upon whose bosom snow has lain;
Who intimately lives with rain.

Poems are made by fools like me,
But only God can make a tree.

FLEAS

By Armand T. Ringer

I think that I shall never see
A poem ugly as a flea.

A flea whose hungry mouth is pressed
Against the flesh upon my chest.

A flea that looks aloft all day
And lifts its little claws to prey.

A flea that may in summer bear
A nest of flealets in my hair.

Upon my bosom it has lain
To intimately cause me pain.

Poems are made by fools like me,
And then are read by fools like thee.

TREES

By Anonymous

I think that I shall never see
A hazard rougher than a tree—

A tree o'er which my ball must fly
If on the green it is to lie;

A tree which stands that green to guard,
And makes the shot extremely hard;

A tree whose leafy arms extend
To kill the mashie shot I send;

A tree that stands in silence there
While angry golfers rave and swear.

Niblicks were made for fools like me,
Who cannot even miss a tree.

18.

If

By Rudyard Kipling

If you can keep your head when all about you
  Are losing theirs and blaming it on you,
If you can trust yourself when all men doubt you,
  But make allowance for their doubting too;
If you can wait and not be tired of waiting,
  Or being lied about, don't deal in lies,
Or being hated don't give way to hating,
  And yet don't look too good, nor talk too wise:

If you can dream—and not make dreams your master;
  If you can think—and not make thoughts your aim,
If you can meet with Triumph and Disaster
  And treat those two impostors just the same;
If you can bear to hear the truth you've spoken
  Twisted by knaves to make a trap for fools,
Or watch the things you gave your life to, broken,
  And stoop and build 'em up with worn-out tools:

If you can make one heap of all your winnings
  And risk it on one turn of pitch-and-toss,
And lose, and start again at your beginnings
  And never breathe a word about your loss;
If you can force your heart and nerve and sinew
  To serve your turn long after they are gone,
And so hold on when there is nothing in you
  Except the Will which says to them: "Hold on!"

If you can talk with crowds and keep your virtue,
    Or walk with Kings—nor lose the common touch,
If neither foes nor loving friends can hurt you,
    If all men count with you, but none too much;
If you can fill the unforgiving minute
    With sixty seconds worth of distance run,
Yours is the Earth and everything that's in it,
    And—which is more—you'll be a Man, my son!

The impulse to write an "If" for girls has been irresistible. At antique shows, I have picked up three such parodies—all framed. The authors are Elizabeth Lincoln Otis, Wilbur D. Nesbit, and J. P. McEvoy. Because they are not comic, I have not included them in this chapter.

IF

By Frank Jacobs, from
Pitiless Parodies and Other Outrageous Verse
(Dover, 1994)

If you can buck a mob of lady shoppers
    And get outside without a scratch or bite;
If you can get a dentist for your choppers
    To fix a toothache on a Sunday night;
If you can smack a truck with your jalopy
    And make the driver think he was to blame;
If you can be a loafer, poor and sloppy,
    Yet have the world think you're some famous name;

If you can change a tire on the thruway,
    While stranded in the busy center lane;
If you can find a foolproof, tried-and-true way
    To housebreak an impossible Great Dane;
If you can find another way to open
    A sardine tin when you have lost the key;

If you can find a fumbled bar of soap in
    Your shower when the suds won't let you see;

If you can rid your house of dull relations
    By faking mumps or plague or Asian flu;
If you can go through tax investigations
    And somehow wind up with them owing you;
If you can read these verses as we list 'em
    And answer "Yes" to each and every one;
Then, Charlie, you have really licked the system—
    And now we wish you'd tell us how it's done.

19.

Tommy

By Rudyard Kipling

I went into a public-'ouse to get a pint o' beer,
The publican 'e up an' sez, "We serve no red-coats here."
The girls be'ind the bar they laughed an' giggled fit to die,
I outs into the street again an' to myself sez I:

> O it's Tommy this, an' Tommy that, an' 'Tommy, go
> away';
> But it's "Thank you, Mister Atkins," when the band
> begins to play,
> The band begins to play, my boys, the band begins to
> play.
> O it's "Thank you, Mister Atkins," when the band begins
> to play.

I went into a theatre as sober as could be,
They gave a drunk civilian room, but 'adn't none for me;
They sent me to the gallery or round the music-'alls,
But when it comes to fightin', Lord! they'll shove me in the stalls!

> For it's Tommy this, an' Tommy that, an' 'Tommy, wait
> outside';
> But it's "Special train for Atkins" when the trooper's on
> the tide,
> The troopship's on the tide, my boys, the troopship's on
> the tide,

O it's "Special train for Atkins" when the trooper's on the
　　tide.

Yes, makin' mock o' uniforms that guard you while you sleep
Is cheaper than them uniforms, an' they're starvation cheap;
An' hustlin' drunken soldiers when they're goin' large a bit
Is five times better business than paradin' in full kit.

　　Then it's Tommy this, an' Tommy that, an 'Tommy, 'ow's
　　　　yer soul?'
　　But it's "Thin red line of 'eroes" when the drums begin to
　　　　roll,
　　The drums begin to roll, my boys, the drums begin to roll,
　　O it's "Thin red line of 'eroes" when the drums begin to
　　　　roll.

We aren't no thin red 'eroes, nor we aren't no blackguards too,
But single men in barricks, most remarkable like you;
An' if sometimes our conduck isn't all your fancy paints:
Why, single men in barricks don't grow into plaster saints;

　　While it's Tommy this, an' Tommy that, an' 'Tommy, fall
　　　　be'ind,'
　　But it's "Please to walk in front, sir," when there's trouble
　　　　in the wind,
　　There's trouble in the wind, my boys, there's trouble in
　　　　the wind,
　　O it's "Please to walk in front, sir," when there's trouble in
　　　　the wind.

You talk o' better food for us, an' schools, an' fires, an' all:
We'll wait for extra rations if you treat us rational.
Don't mess about the cook-room slops, but prove it to our face
The Widow's Uniform is not the soldier-man's disgrace.

> For it's Tommy this, an' Tommy that, an' "Chuck him out,
>   the brute!"
> But it's "Saviour of 'is country," when the guns begin to
>   shoot;
> Yes it's Tommy this, an' Tommy that, an' anything you
>   please;
> But Tommy ain't a bloomin' fool—you bet that Tommy
>   sees!

HUCKSTER

By Rollie Abrahams,
from **Printer's Ink** *(January 23, 1953)*

I walked into a Men's Club for a half a drop, of cheer.
The steward shook his nose and said, "We serve no salesmen
    here,"
The men behind the armchairs humphed and snorted fit to die.
I outs into the street again, and to myself says I:

> O, it's huckster this and huckster that and huckster, go
>   away,
> But it's "Thank you, Mr. Adman" when the ads begin to
>   pay.
> The ads begin to pay, boys, the ads begin to pay . . .
> Then it's "Thank you, Mr. Adman" when the ads begin to
>   pay.

I stepped into a lecture hall to hear a bit of sense.
A college prof is steaming off in learned eloquence.
He's saying, "Advertising is a tool for men of greed
To make the people spend their dough on things they do not
    need."

Yes, it's huckster this and huckster that and huckster, you
    don't count.
(But we make for better products when the facts begin to
    mount.)
The facts begin to mount, boys, the facts begin to
    mount . . .
Then it's "higher living standard" when the facts begin to
    mount.

The idealistic editor is crying in his cups
That he has to slant his stories for those advertising pups.
He can't think of an instance, but he knows the danger's near,
For the ads pay for his writers, his production-and his beer!

So it's huckster this and huckster that and huckster, spare
    my door!
But it's "Get another page in" when the presses start to
    roar.
The presses start to roar, boys, the presses start to roar . . .
It's "Ads have made our paper big," when presses start to
    roar.

The family's seated cozily around the TV set
Enjoying top flight comedy or music from the Met.
To pay for theater seats when they've got this would be absurd,
But it's "Damn-those damn-commercials" when the sponsor
    says a word.

For it's huckster this and huckster that and huckster,
    you're a bore.
But it's "Get the game on TV, boys, I want to know the
    score.
I want to know the score, boys." (If he wants to know the
    score,
The admen make the shows for him, if he wants to know
    the score.)

When Mother goes out shopping, she is careful of her brands.
The ads have told her what is good in words she understands.
They've mentioned the ingredients, the uses and the price—
But Father says, "Before you buy a famous brand, think twice."

> For it's huckster this and huckster that and "Darling, use
> your head.
> You pay for advertising when you buy that kind of
> bread."
> But it costs her no more money when she buys that kind
> of bread . . .
> Ads make for mass production, keeping prices down
> instead.

Yes, they call us "eager beavers" and they sometimes call us
"crooks,"
And they laugh at us in comedies and damn us in their books.
We're the scapegoats of the business world and brash fifteen
percenters,
We're Fascists, faddists, phonies, and at best we're hoax
inventors.

We know we're sometimes upstarts, and we know we're in
our youth
But we've got to entertain them and we've got to tell the truth.
They know we do a job for them, in our own peculiar way . . .
And it's "Thank you, Mr. Adman" when the ads begin to pay.

20.

GUNGA DIN

By Rudyard Kipling

You may talk o' gin and beer
When you're quartered safe out 'ere,
An' you're sent to penny-fights an' Aldershot it;
But when it comes to slaughter
You will do your work on water,
An' you'll lick the bloomin' boots of 'im that's got it.
Now in Injia's sunny clime,
Where I used to spend my time
A-servin' of 'Er Majesty the Queen,
Of all them blackfaced crew
The finest man I knew
Was our regimental bhisti, Gunga Din.
      He was 'Din! Din! Din!
      You limping lump o' brick-dust, Gunga Din!
      Hi! slippery hitherao!
      Water, get it! Pancee lao!
      You squidgy-nosed old idol, Gunga Din.'

The uniform 'e wore
Was nothin' much before,
An' rather less than 'arf o' that be'ind,
For a piece o' twisty rag
An' a goatskin water-bag
Was all the field-equipment 'e could find.
When the sweatin' troop-train lay
In a sidin' through the day,

Where the 'eat would make your bloomin' eyebrows crawl,
We shouted "Harry By!"
Till our throats were bricky-dry,
Then we wopped 'im 'cause 'e couldn't serve us all.
   It was "Din! Din! Din!
   You 'eathen, where the mischief 'ave you been?
   You put some juldee in it
   Or I'll marrow you this minute
   If you don't fill up my helmet, Gunga Din!"

   'E would dot an' carry one
   Till the longest day was done;
An' 'e didn't seem to know the use o' fear.
   If we charged or broke or cut,
   You could bet your bloomin' nut,
'E'd be waitin' fifty paces right flank rear.
   With 'is mussick on 'is back,
   'E would skip with our attack,
An' watch us till the bugles made "Retire,"
   An' for all 'is dirty 'ide
   'E was white, clear white, inside
When 'e went to tend the wounded under fire!
   It was "Din! Din! Din!"
  With the bullets kickin' dust-spots on the green.
   When the cartridges ran out,
   You could hear the front-files shout,
  "Hi! ammunition-mules an' Gunga Din!"
   I sha'n't forgit the night
   When I dropped be'ind the fight
With a bullet where my belt-plate should 'a' been.
   I was chokin' mad with thirst,
   An' the man that spied me first
Was our good old grinnin', gruntin' Gunga Din.
   'E lifted up my 'ead,
   An' he plugged me where I bled,
An' 'e guv me 'arf-a-pint o' water-green:

It was crawlin' and it stunk,
But of all the drinks I've drunk,
I'm gratefullest to one from Gunga Din.
    It was "Din! Din! Din!"
'Ere's a beggar with a bullet through 'is spleen;
    'E's chawin' up the ground,
    An' 'e's kickin' all around:
For Gawd's sake git the water, Gunga Din!

'E carried me away
To where a dooli lay,
An' a bullet come an' drilled the beggar clean.
    'E put me safe inside,
    An' just before 'e died:
"I 'ope you liked your drink," sez Gunga Din.
    So I'll meet 'im later on
    At the place where 'e is gone—
Where it's always double drill and no canteen;
    'E'll be squattin' on the coals,
    Givin' drink to poor damned souls,
An' I'll get a swig in hell from Gunga Din!
        Yes, Din! Din! Din!
    You Lazarushian-leather Gunga Din!
        Though I've belted you and flayed you,
        By the living Gawd that made you,
    You're a better man than I am, Gunga Din!

GUNGA DEAN

By Rollie Abrahams

You may talk of gin and beer,
But you cannot keep it near,
Or the proctor's apt to visit you and find it.
So each thirsty son and daughter
Has to do his work on water
Or get drunk so far away no one will mind it.
For in Syracuse's clime
You are not to spend your time
In drinking till you turn a ghastly green,
Since as sure as drink is sin
Some abstainer will break in
And you'll find that you are up before the dean.
For it's "Dean, Dean, Dean,
'Twas only just a little grenadine.
    And whatever do you think
    I could do on just one drink?
And other guys keep bottles, but unseen."

The coeds dungarees,
Which are rolled above their knees
And frequently are worn with T-shirts tight,
Suggest some outdoor fun,
Which is usually done
On the campus in the afternoon or night,
For it's very nice to pass
Those few minutes after class
With a bit of friendly necking on the green,
But the faculty will frown
On a lady's lying down
And will quickly send her off to see the dean.
And it's "Dean, Dean, Dean,
I hope you know my character is clean,

But at times I'm not so sure
    All the good in life is pure . . .
I'm sure you know exactly what I mean."

You're allowed three cuts a term,
And instructors will be firm
In demanding notes each time you overcut;
For they say if they permit
Attending class when you see fit,
The faculty will get into a rut,
Furthermore, twelve cuts will force
Them to fail you in the course—
Which action you'll consider very mean,
And more so when you see
That your final mark was B.
So you scamper to the office of the dean.
And it's "Dean, Dean, Dean,
My record always has been high and clean.
    My instructor was a bore
    I could not stand any more.
That I knew the work is plainly to be seen."

Now a student's aim in class
Is essentially to pass
And if lie discovers that he's in the dark
And his brain is all confused
With his honor points all used,
It will soon be clear that he has missed his mark.
But a fellow's not undone
If he doesn't average 1.0
And his punishment won't make him pale and lean.
But a co-ed on probation
Has a nasty situation
And soon she'll pay a visit to the dean.
And it's, "Dean, Dean, Dean,"
(While she sweetly smiles and dimples in between)

"I know that I'm on pro,
But I'm going steady, so
I simply can't be in by nine-fifteen."

The waiting room is full
Of the type who has the pull,
As his uncle knows a friend of Harry Truman.
So he thinks the college savors
Every chance to do him favors.
It's enough to break the heart of any human.
So with lateness and with cuts
And with *pleases* and with *buts*
For every aspect of the college scene,
There is one man who is sought—
To whom all complaints are brought . . .
I can hear them shouting, "Tell it to the dean!"
Dean! Dean! Dean!
What a nightmare this semester must have been.
Though I've kidded and declaimed you
I have never really blamed you.
You're a better man than I am, mister Dean!

21.

EXCELSIOR

By Henry Wadsworth Longfellow

The shades of night were falling fast,
As through an Alpine village passed
A youth, who bore, 'mid snow and ice,
A banner with the strange device,
      Excelsior!

His brow was sad; his eye beneath,
Flashed like a falchion from its sheath,
And like a silver clarion rung
The accents of that unknown tongue,
      Excelsior!

In happy homes he saw the light
Of household fires gleam warm and bright;
Above, the spectral glaciers shone,
And from his lips escaped a groan,
      Excelsior!

"Try not the Pass!" the old man said;
"Dark lowers the tempest overhead,
The roaring torrent is deep and wide!"
And loud that clarion voice replied,
      Excelsior!

"Oh stay," the maiden said, "and rest
Thy weary head upon this breast!"

A tear stood in his bright blue eye,
But still he answered, with a sigh,
            Excelsior!

"Beware the pine-tree's withered branch!
Beware the awful avalanche!"
This was the peasant's last Good-night,
A voice replied, far up the height,
            Excelsior!

At break of day, as heavenward
The pious monks of Saint Bernard
Uttered the oft-repeated prayer,
A voice cried through the startled air,
            Excelsior!

A traveller, by the faithful hound,
Half-buried in the snow was found,
Still grasping in his hand of ice
That banner with the strange device,
            Excelsior!

There in the twilight cold and gray,
Lifeless, but beautiful, he lay,
And from the sky, serene and far,
A voice fell, like a failing star,
            Excelsior!

Pat's Excelsior

By Anonymous

'Twas growin' dark so terrible fasht,
Whin through a town up the mountain there pashed
A broth of a boy, to his neck in the shnow;

As he walked, his shillaleh he swung to and fro,
Saying: "It's up to the top I am bound for to go,
   Be jabbers!"

He looked mortal sad, and his eye was as bright
As a fire of turf on a cowld winther night;
And nivir a word that he said could ye tell
As he opened his mouth and let out a yell,
"It's up till the top of the mountain I'll go,
Onless covered up wid this bodthersome shnow
   Be jabbers!"

Through the windows he saw, as he thraveled along,
The light of the candles and fires so warm,
But a big chunk of ice hung over his head;
Wid a shnivel and groan, "By St. Patrick!" he said,
"It's up to the very *tip-top* I will rush,
And then if it falls, it's not meself it'll crush,
   Be jabbers!"

"Whisht a bit," said an owld man, whose hair was white
As the shnow that fell down on that miserable night;
"Shure ye'll fall in the wather, me bit of a lad
Fur the night is so dark and the walkin' is bad."
Bedad! he'd not lisht to a word that was said,
But he'd go to the top, if he went on his head,
   Be jabbers!

A bright, buxom young girl, such as likes to be kissed,
Axed him wouldn' he stop, and how *could* he resist?
So shnapping his fingers and winking his eye,
While shmiling upon her, he made this reply—
"Faith, I meant to kape on till I got to the top,
But, as yer shwate self axed me, I may as well shtop,
   Be jabbers!"

He shtopped all night and he shtopped all day—
And ye mustn't be axin whin he did go away;
Fur wouldn't he be a bastely gossoon
To be lavin his darlint in the swate honeymoon?
Whin the owld man has his praties enough and to spare,
Shure he might as well shtay if he's comfortable, there
                    Be jabbers!

HIGHER

By Anonymous

The shadows of night were a-comin' down swift,
And the dazzlin' snow lay drift on drift,
As thro' a village a youth did go,
A-carryin' a flag with this motto—
                    Higher!

O'er a forehead high curled copious hair,
His nose a Roman, complexion fair,
O'er an eagle eye an auburn lash,
And be never stopped shoutin' thro' his mustache,
                    "Higher!"

He saw thro' the windows as be kept gettin' upper
A number of families sittin' at supper,
But be eyes the slippery rocks very keen
And fled as he cried, and cried while a-fleein'—
                    "Higher!"

"Take care you there!" said an old woman; "stop!
It's blowing gales up there on top—
You'll tumble off on t' other side!"
But the hurryin' stranger loud replied,
                    "Higher!"

"Oh! don't you go up such a shocking night,
Come sleep on my lap," said a maiden bright.
On his Roman nose a teardrop come,
But still he remarked, as he upward clomb,
            "Higher!"

"Look out for the branch of that sycamore tree!
Dodge rolling stones, if any you see!"
Sayin' which the farmer went home to bed
And the singular voice replied overhead,
            "Higher!"

About quarter past six the next afternoon,
A man accidentally goin' up soon,
Heard spoken above him as often as twice
The very same word in a very weak voice,
            "Higher!"

And not far, I believe, from quarter of seven—
He was slow gettin' up, the road bein' uneven—
Found the stranger dead in the drifted snow,
Still clutchin' the flag with the motto—
            Higher!

Yes! lifeless, defunct, without any doubt,
The lamp of life being decidedly out,
On the dreary hillside the youth was a-layin'!
And there was no more use for him to be sayin'
            "Higher!"

EXCELSIOR

By Anonymous

The swampy State of Illinois
      Contained a greenish sort of boy,

Who read with idiotic joy—
    "Excelsior!"

He tarried not to eat or drink,
    But put a flag of lightish pink,
    And traced on it in violet ink—
        Excelsior!

Though what he meant by that absurd,
    Uncouth, and stupid, senseless word,
    Has not been placed upon record—
        Excelsior!

The characters were very plain,
    In German text, yet he was fain
    With greater clearness to explain—
        Excelsior!

And so he ran, this stupid wight,
    And hollered out with all his might,
    (As to a person out of sight)—
        "Excelsior!"

And everybody thought the lad
    Within an ace of being mad,
    Who cried in accents stern and sad—
        "Excelsior!"

"Come to my arms," the maiden cried;
    The youth grinned sheepishly, and sighed,
    And then appropriately replied—
        "Excelsior!"

The evening sun is in the sky,
    But still the creature mounts on high
    And shouts (nor gives a reason why)
        "Excelsior!"

And ere he gains the topmost crag
   His feeble legs begin to lag;
    Unsteadily lie holds the flag—
      Excelsior!

Now P.C. Nab is on his track!
   He puts him in an empty sack,
    And brings him home upon his back—
      Excelsior!

Nab takes him to a lumber store,
   They toss him in and lock the door,
    Which only makes him bawl the more—
      "Excelsior!"

THE SHADES OF NIGHT

By A. E. Houseman

The shades of night were falling fast,
   And the rain was falling faster,
When through an Alpine village passed
   An Alpine village pastor:
A youth who bore mid snow and ice
   A bird that wouldn't chirrup,
And a banner with the strange device—
   "Mrs. Winslow's soothing syrup."

"Beware the pass," the old man said,
   "My bold, my desperate fellah;
Dark lowers the tempest overhead,
   And you'll want your umbrella;
And the roaring torrent is deep and wide—
   You may hear how loud it washes."
But still that clarion voice replied:
   "I've got my old goloshes."

"Oh, stay," the maiden said, "and rest
   (For the wind blows from the nor'ward)
Thy weary head upon my breast—
   And please don't think I'm forward."
A tear stood in his bright blue eye,
   And he gladly would have tarried;
But still he answered with a sigh:
   "Unhappily I'm married."

Franklin P. Adams, in **Something Else Again,** *imagines how newspaper copy might have handled the "Excelsior" story:*

DOG FINDS LAD
DEAD IN DRIFT

Unidentified: Body of Young Traveler
Found by Faithful Hound Near
Small Alpine Village—White
Mantle His Snowy Shroud

ST. BERNARD, Sept. 12.—Early this morning a dog belonging to the St. Bernard Monastery discovered the body of a young man, half buried in the snow.

In his hand was clutched a flag with the word "Excelsior" printed on it.

It is thought that he passed through the village last night, bearing the banner, and that a young woman had offered him shelter, which he refused, having answered "Excelsior."

The police are working on the case.

22.

HIAWATHA

By Henry Wadsworth Longfellow

This poem is much too long to quote, but the short parody that follows is too funny to omit. Incidentally, Lewis Carroll wrote a lengthy parody titled "Hiawatha's Photographing." It can be found in the Dover paperback, *The Humorous Verse of Lewis Carroll*.

Henry Wadsworth Longfellow

THE MODERN HIAWATHA

By George A. Strong

He killed the noble Mudjokivis.
Of the skin he made him mittens,
Made them with the fur side inside,
Made them with the skin side outside.
He, to get the warm side inside,
Put the inside skin side outside;
He, to get the cold side outside,
Put the warm side fur side inside.

That's why he put the fur side inside,
Why he put the skin side outside,
Why he turned them inside outside.

23

THE VILLAGE BLACKSMITH

By Henry Wadsworth Longfellow

Under a spreading chestnut-tree
    The village smithy stands;
The smith, a mighty man is he,
    With large and sinewy hands;
And the muscles of his brawny arms
    Are strong as iron bands.

His hair is crisp, and black, and long,
    His face is like the tan;
His brow is wet with honest sweat,
    He earns whate'er he can,
And looks the whole world in the face,
    For he owes not any man.

Week in, week out, from morn till night,
    You can hear his bellows blow;
You can hear him swing his heavy sledge,
    With measured beat and slow,
Like a sexton ringing the village bell,
    When the evening sun is low.

And children coming home from school
    Look in at the open door;
They love to see the flaming forge,
    And hear the bellows roar,

"The smith, a mighty man is he."

And catch the burning sparks that fly
    Like chaff from a threshing-floor.

He goes on Sunday to the church,
    And sits among his boys;
He hears the parson pray and preach,
    He hears his daughter's voice,
Singing in the village choir,
    And it makes his heart rejoice.

It sounds to him like her mother's voice,
    Singing in Paradise!
He needs must think of her once more,
    How in the grave she lies;
And with his hard, rough hand he wipes
    A tear out of his eyes.

Toiling,—rejoicing,—sorrowing,
    Onward through life he goes;
Each morning sees some task begin,
    Each evening sees it close;
Something attempted, something done,
    Has earned a night's repose.

Thanks, thanks to thee, my worthy friend,
    For the lesson thou hast taught!
Thus at the flaming forge of life
    Our fortunes must be wrought;
Thus on its sounding anvil shaped
    Each burning deed and thought.

THE VILLAGE HIPPIE

By Frank Jacobs,
from **Pitiless Parodies and Other Outrageous Verse**
(Dover 1994)

Under his pad on 10th and B
    The Village Hippie stands;
A turned-on acid-head is he
    With pale and shaking hands;
And the flower jacket that he wears
    Hangs down in tattered strands.

His hair is long and blonde and curled;
    He sets it when he can;
His face is caked with unwashed grime
    That looks just like a tan;
And when he's near, you sort of wish
    He'd use Right Guard or Ban.

His pad is but a place for him
    To freak out in a crash;

The mouldy mattress on the floor
     Contains his secret stash—
In case the Narcs come busting in
     To glom his pot and hash.

His roomies, high on boo and coke,
     Are fogged in smoky swirls;
And as the Hippie tunes in on
     Their dungarees and curls,
He thinks it might be possible
     That some of them are girls.

No hang-ups bug his spaced-out world;
     He has no pressing need;
Last night he flew on LSD;
     Tonight he'll cop a weed;
Tomorrow he'll flip out of sight
     And blow his mind on speed.

The years fly by, and now let's see
     The Hippie we once knew;
His hair's turned white; his teeth are gone;
     His mind is rotted through;
Who ever thought he'd live to reach
     The age of thirty-two?

The Minnesota Wrestler

By Armand T. Ringer

Under the spreading repartee
     The St. Paul wrestler stands.
The "Body," a mighty man is he,
     With large and sinewy hands;
And the muscles of his brawny arms
     Are strong as iron bands.

Ventura's hair, once black and long,
    Departed long ago;
His brow was wet with honest sweat
    When he worked as a wrestling pro.
Opponents get the hammerlock.
    He fears not any foe.

Reporters coming home from work
    Look in through his open door.
They love to see his biceps bulge,
    And hear his bellows roar,
And catch the crafty spins that fly
    Like lies on the senate floor.

Ventura never goes to church.
    Religion's not for him.
He much prefers to stay at home,
    And pump iron in his gym.
But faith, he grants, gives comfort to
    Poor souls whose wits are dim.

Toiling, rejoicing, blustering,
    On through his term he goes,
Proposing this, reforming that,
    But will they work? Who knows?
It's slouching toward the White House that
    Keeps Jesse on his toes.

Thanks, thanks to thee, my awesome friend,
    For the lessons thou hast taught;
That on the wrestling mat of life
    Our fortunes must be wrought,
And one can rise in politics
    Without a serious thought.

24.

THE DAY IS DONE

By Henry Wadsworth Longfellow

The day is done, and the darkness
  Falls from the wings of Night,
As a feather is wafted downward
  From an eagle in his flight.

I see the lights of the village
  Gleam through the rain and the mist,
And a feeling of sadness comes o'er me
  That my soul cannot resist:

A feeling of sadness and longing,
  That is not akin to pain,
And resembles sorrow only
  As the mist resembles the rain.

Come, read to me some poem,
  Some simple and heartfelt lay,
That shall soothe this restless feeling,
  And banish the thoughts of day.

Not from the grand old masters,
  Not from the bards sublime,
Whose distant footsteps echo
  Through the corridors of Time.

For, like strains of martial music,
    Their mighty thoughts suggest
Life's endless toil and endeavor;
    And to-night I long for rest.

Read from some humbler poet,
    Whose songs gushed from his heart,
As showers from the clouds of summer,
    Or tears from the eyelids start;

Who, through long days of labor,
    And nights devoid of ease,
Still heard in his soul the music
    Of wonderful melodies.

Such songs have power to quiet
    The restless pulse of care,
And come like the benediction
    That follows after prayer.

Then read from the treasured volume
    The poem of thy choice,
And lend to the rhyme of the poet
    The beauty of thy voice.

And the night shall be filled with music,
    And the cares, that infest the day,
Shall fold their tents, like the Arabs,
    And as silently steal away.

THE DAY IS DONE

By Phoebe Cary

The day is done, and darkness
    From the wing of night is loosed,
As a feather is wafted downward,
    From a chicken going to roost.

I see the lights of the baker,
    Gleam through the rain and mist,
And a feeling of sadness comes o'er me,
    That I cannot well resist.

A feeling of sadness and longing
    That is not like being sick,
And resembles sorrow only
    As a brickbat resembles a brick.

Come, get for me some supper,—
    A good and regular meal—
That shall soothe this restless feeling,
    And banish the pain I feel.

Not from the pastry bakers,
    Not from the shops for cake;
I would n't give a farthing
    For all that they can make.

For, like the soup at dinner,
    Such things would but suggest
Some dishes more substantial,
    And to-night I want the best.

Go to some honest butcher,
    Whose beef is fresh and nice,

As any they have in the city,
    And get a liberal slice.

Such things through days of labor,
    And nights devoid of ease,
For sad and desperate feelings,
    Are wonderful remedies.

They have an astonishing power
    To aid and reinforce,
And come like the "finally, brethren,"
    That follows a long discourse.

Then get me a tender sirloin
    From off the bench or hook.
And lend to its sterling goodness
    The science of the cook.

And the night shall be filled with comfort,
    And the cares with which it begun
Shall fold up their blankets like Indians,
    And silently cut and run.

25.

A PSALM OF LIFE

By Henry Wadsworth Longfellow

Tell me not, in mournful numbers,
    Life is but an empty dream!—
For the soul is dead that slumbers,
    And things are not what they seem.

Life is real! Life is earnest!
    And the grave is not its goal;
Dust thou art, to dust returnest,
    Was not spoken of the soul.

Not enjoyment, and not sorrow,
    Is our destined end or way;
But to act, that each to-morrow
    Find us farther than to-day.

Art is long, and Time is fleeting,
    And our hearts, though stout and brave,
Still, like muffled drums, are beating
    Funeral marches to the grave.

In the world's broad field of battle,
    In the bivouac of Life,
Be not like dumb, driven cattle!
    Be a hero in the strife!

Trust no Future, howe'er pleasant!
    Let the dead Past bury its dead!
Act,—act in the living Present!
    Heart within, and God o'erhead!

Lives of great men all remind us
    We can make our lives sublime,
And, departing, leave behind us
    Footprints on the sands of time;

Footprints, that perhaps another,
    Sailing o'er life's solemn main,
A forlorn and shipwrecked brother,
    Seeing, shall take heart again.

Let us, then, be up and doing,
    With a heart for any fate;
Still achieving, still pursuing,
    Learn to labor and to wait.

A PSALM OF LABORING LIFE

By Franklin P. Adams, in Something Else Again (1920)

Tell me not, in doctored numbers,
    Life is but a name for work!
For the labour that encumbers
    Me I wish that I could shirk.

Life is phony! Life is rotten!
    And the wealthy have no soul;
Why should you be picking cotton?
    Why should I be mining coal?

Not employment and not sorrow
    Is my destined end or way;
But to act that each to-morrow
    Finds me idler than to-day.

Work is long, and plutes are lunching;
    Money is the thing I crave;
But my heart continues punching
    Funeral time-clocks to the grave.

In the world's uneven battle,
    In the swindle known as life,
Be not like the stockyards cattle—
    Stick your partner with a knife!

Trust no Boss, however pleasant!
    Capital is but a curse!
Strike,—strike in the living present!
    Fill, oh fill, the bulging purse!

Lives of strikers all remind us
    We can make our lives a crime,
And, departing, leave behind us
    Bills for double overtime.

Charges that, perhaps another,
    Working for a stingy ten
Bucks a day, some mining brother
    Seeing, shall walk out again.

Let us, then, be up and striking,
    Discontent with all of it;
Still undoing, still disliking,
    Learn to labour—and to quit.

Psalm of the Baldhead

By Anonymous

I found this in an old scrapbook that credited it to the *Boston Transcript*, but gave no date or author.

Tell me not, in, merry accents,
    That I have an unthatched roof;
'Tis the hairy head that lacks sense—
    Baldness is of thought a proof.

Hair is vulgar, hair is useless,
    And to brush and comb's a bore,
Making life but dull and juiceless
    I need brush and comb no more.

Not for wise men matted hair is,
    Black or brown or red or fair;
Let the savage of the prairies
    Waste his time in raising hair!

Life is short, and hairs are numbered,
    And, though flies are hardly borne,
Still at night I've always slumbered,
    When the night-cap I have worn.

Is the world's broad field of battle,
    Who'd be at the barber's call,
Listening to his tiresome tattle,
    Better bare as billiard ball!

Fear no future, baldhead brother,
    You were bald in infant days;
Crave not hirsute of another—
    Brain it is, not hair that pays.

Lives of great men all remind us
    That our smooth and polished pates
Leave all hairy heads behind us—
    Let us thank the favoring fates!

Foot-prints of Old Time's fleet walking
    No one sees on our smooth crowns,
Mind no more the Idle talking
    Made by envious mop-head clowns.

Let us, then, O hairless brother,
    Proudly through life's pathway roll;
We remember that dear mother
    Earth is barren at the pole.

A PSALM OF LIFE

By Phoebe Cary

Tell me not in idle jingle,
    "Marriage is an empty dream!"
For the girl is dead that's single,
    And girls are not what they seem.

Life is real! Life is earnest!
    Single blessedness a fib!
"Man thou art, to man returnest!"
    Has been spoken of the rib.

Not enjoyment, and not sorrow,
    Is our destined end or way;
But to act that each to-morrow
    Finds us nearer marriage day.

Life is long, and youth is fleeting,
    And our hearts, though light and gay,
Still like pleasant drums are beating
    Wedding marches all the way.

In the world's broad field of battle,
    In the bivouac of life,
Be not like dumb driven cattle!
    Be a heroine—a wife!—

Trust no future, howe'er pleasant,
    Let the dead past bury its dead!
Act—act to the living Present!
    Heart within and hope ahead!

Lives of married folks remind us
    We can live our lives as well,
And, departing, leave behind us
    Such examples as shall "tell."

Such example that another,
    Wasting time in idle sport,
A forlorn, unmarried brother,
    Seeing, shall take heart and court.

Let us, then be up and doing,
    With a heart on triumph set
Still contriving, still pursuing,
    And each one a husband get.

26.

THE ARROW AND THE SONG

By Henry Wadsworth Longfellow

I shot an arrow into the air,
It fell to earth, I knew not where;
For, so swiftly it flew, the sight
Could not follow it in its flight.

I breathed a song into the air,
It fell to earth, I knew not where;
For who has sight so keen and strong,
That it can follow the flight of song?

Long, long afterward, in an oak
I found the arrow, still unbroke;
And the song, from beginning to end,
I found again in the heart of a friend.

THE ARROW

By D. B. Wyndham Lewis

I shot an arrow into the air:
I don't know how it fell or where;
But strangely enough, at my journey's end,
I found it again in the neck of a friend.

LOST ARROWS

By Anonymous

I shot an arrow into the air.
It fell to earth I know not where.
I lost a lot of arrows that way.

27.

MY CANDLE

By Edna St. Vincent Millay

My candle burns at both ends;
    It will not last the night;
But ah, my foes and oh, my friends—
    It gives a lovely light.

MY CANDLE

By Rod Maclean

My candle burns at both ends;
    It will not last the night;
But while it's fit, you must admit
    It saves electric light.

28.

News Item

By Dorothy Parker

Men seldom make passes
At girls who wear glasses

The following Corrections 2 through 4 are from *The Random House Treasury of Light Verse*, edited by Louis Phillips.

Correction 1

By Ogden Nash

Girls who are bespectacled
Sometimes have their neck tickled

Correction 2

By Dorothy Dreher

Men often lose their senses
Over girls with contact lenses

CORRECTION 3

By Anonymous

I heard a woman mutter:
Glasses or no glasses,
It neither hinders nor hurts,
For men will make passes
At anything in skirts.

CORRECTION 4

By Bob McKenty

Men often get amorous
With gals who are mammarous.

29.

The Bells

By Edgar Allan Poe

I

Hear the sledges with the bells—
Silver bells!
What a world of merriment their melody foretells!
How they tinkle, tinkle, tinkle,
In the icy air of night!
While the stars that oversprinkle
All the heavens, seem to twinkle
With a crystalline delight;
Keeping time, time, time,
In a sort of Runic rhyme,
To the tintinnabulation that so musically wells
From the bells, bells, bells, bells,
Bells, bells, bells—
From the jingling and tinkling of the bells.

II

Hear the mellow wedding bells—
Golden bells!
What a world of happiness their harmony foretells!
Through the balmy air of night
How they ring out their delight!—
From the molten-golden notes,

And all in tune,
What a liquid ditty floats
To the turtle-dove that listens, while she gloats
On the moon!
Oh, from out the sounding cells,
What a gush of euphony voluminously wells!
How it swells!
How it dwells
On the Future!—how it tells
Of the rapture that impels
To the swinging and the ringing
Of the bells, bells, bells—
Of the bells, bells, bells, bells,
Bells, bells, bells—
To the rhyming and the chiming of the bells!

III

Hear the loud alarum bells—
Brazen bells!
What a tale of terror, now their turbulency tells!
In the startled ear of night
How they scream out their affright!
Too much horrified to speak,
They can only shriek, shriek,
Out of tune,
In a clamorous appealing to the mercy of the fire,
In a mad expostulation with the deaf and frantic fire,
Leaping higher, higher, higher,
With a desperate desire,
And a resolute endeavour
Now—now to sit, or never,
By the side of the pale-faced moon.
Oh, the bells, bells, bells!
What a tale their terror tells
Of Despair!

How they clang, and clash, and roar!
What a horror they outpour
On the bosom of the palpitating air!
Yet the ear, it fully knows,
By the twanging,
And the clanging,
How the danger ebbs and flows;
Yet the ear distinctly tells,
In the jangling,
And the wrangling,
How the danger sinks and swells,
By the sinking or the swelling in the anger of the bells—
Of the bells—
Of the bells, bells, bells, bells,
Bells, bells, bells—
In the clamor and the clanging of the bells!

IV

Hear the tolling of the bells—
Iron bells!
What a word of solemn thought their monody compels!
In the silence of the night,
How we shiver with affright
At the melancholy menace of their tone!
For every sound that floats
From the rust within their throats
Is a groan.
And the people—ah, the people—
They that dwell up in the steeple,
All alone,
And who, tolling, tolling, tolling,
In that muffled monotone,
Feel a glory in so rolling
On the human heart a stone—
They are neither man nor woman—

They are neither brute nor human—
  They are Ghouls:—
And their king it is who tolls:—
And he rolls, rolls, rolls,
   Rolls
A pæan from the bells!
And his merry bosom swells
With the pæan of the bells!
And he dances, and he yells;
 Keeping time, time, time,
 In a sort of Runic rhyme,
  To the pæan of the bells:—
   Of the bells:—
 Keeping time, time, time
 In a sort of Runic rhyme,
  To the throbbing of the bells—
  Of the bells, bells, bells:—
To the sobbing of the bells:—
Keeping time, time, time,
  As he knells, knells, knells,
 In a happy Runic rhyme,
   To the rolling of the bells—
   Of the bells, bells, bells:—
   To the tolling of the bells—
 Of the bells, bells, bells, bells,
  Bells, bells, bells—
To the moaning and the groaning of the bells.

THE BALLS

By Ashleigh Brilliant, from his
Be a Good Neighbor and Leave Me Alone *(1992)*

Hear the rackets with the balls—
Tennis balls!
What a world of merriment their melody recalls!
How they bounce, bounce, bounce,
On the green and grassy court
While the sun burns down with power
Onto every leaf and flower
—What a fascinating sport!
In the beat, beat, beat,
Of the searing summer heat,
While the semi-apathetic watchers lean against the walls
Watching balls, balls, balls, balls
Balls, balls, balls—
Watch the bouncing and the trouncing of the balls.

Hear the rolling of the balls—
Bowling balls!
What a world of wonderment their gravity enthralls!
How they rumble, rumble, rumble
Down the shiny bowling lane—
You must never stop or stumble
With your body or your brain
As you bowl, bowl, bowl,
With your heart and with your soul
For the sake of every skittle that inevitably falls
To the balls, balls, balls, balls
Balls, balls, balls—
To the crashing and the bashing of the balls.

Hear the pinging of the balls—
Ping-pong balls!

What a world of happiness their rhapsody recalls!
     In a large and hollow room
               How they banish all the gloom
     As they echo to the impact
     Of a chop;
               What a sweet stacatto soars
          To re-echo on the ceiling and the floors
          Till they stop;
Bounding from a table flat,
          What a happy way of giving tit-for-tat
               With a pat
               Of your bat
          Your opponent murmers "Drat!"
          And you know that that is that;
          You have won another battle
          With the balls, balls, balls,
     With the balls, balls, balls, balls,
               Balls, balls, balls—

THE FLUTE

By Anonymous

          Hear the fluter with his flute,
               Silver flute!
Oh, what a world of wailing is awakened by its toot!
          How it demi-semi quavers
               On the maddened air of night!
          And defieth all endeavors
               To escape the sound or sigh
          Of the flute, flute, flute,
          With its tootle, tootle, toot;
With reiterated tooteling of exasperating toots,
The long protracted tootelings of agonizing toots
          Of the flute, flute, flute, flute,

Flute, flute, flute,
And the wheezings and the spittings of its toots.
Should he get that other flute,
Golden flute,
Oh, what a deeper anguish will his presence institoot!
How his eyes to heaven he'll raise,
As he plays,
All the days!
How he'll stop us on our ways
With its praise!
And the people—oh, the people,
That don't live up in the steeple,
But inhabit Christian parlors
Where he visiteth and plays,
Where he plays, plays, plays
In the cruellest of ways,
And thinks we ought to listen,
And expects us to be mute,
Who would rather have the earache
Than the music of his flute,
Of his flute, flute, flute,
And the tootings of his toot,
Of the toots wherewith he tooteleth its agonizing toot,
Of the flute, flewt, fluit, floot,
Phlute, phlewt, phlewght,
And the tootle, tootle, tooting of its toot.

SOME OTHER BELLS

By "Teacher," in the Richmond Dispatch (December 25, 1881)

Hear the ringing of the bells!
Jangling bells!
What a world of misery their brazen clang foretells

When they jingle, jingle, jingle
In the icy air of morn!
How our shuddering nerves do tingle
As their rude tones intermingle
With the chanticleer's horn!
Oh, those hated rising bells!
What a world of misery their startling clang foretells
When from couches soft and warm,
And sweet dreams that soothe and charm,
They call us to life's labors and its cares,
To the torments and the worries and the jars
That assail us with the light
And pursue us till the night.

Hear the tinkling of the bells,
Doleful bells!
What a world of dreary toil their monody compels
As they call us into school!
How the ruler and the ruled
Do shudder at the menace of their tone.
Yes, every sound that floats
From their hollow, brazen throats
Is a groan.

Oh! the bells, school-bells!
What infinite vexation their dreary clang foretells
Of the noisy little monkeys
And the stupid little donkeys,
With their countless tricks and pranks,
And their countless kinks and cranks—
Of the Spellers greased and torn,
And the Readers soiled and worn—
Of subtraction and addition,
And the fearful "composition,"
With its hieroglyphics telling,
In its crude, phonetic spelling,

The wildest, queerest fictions,
The absurdest contradictions. . . .
Oh the bells! bells! bells!
Brazen bells!
What a day of dreary toil their dismal clang foretells!

THE PHONE

By Frank Jacobs, from Mad for Better or Verse (Warner, 1975)

See the salesman on the phone—
Public phone!
Calling Minnesota on a deal he can't postpone!
Ah, what anger he is feeling
As he tries to make his call!
Hear him bellowing and squealing
'Cause he's reached a bar in Wheeling
When he thought he had St. Paul!
Hear him shout, shout, shout
That his quarters have run out—
That he's lost the operator and can't get a dial tone!
On the phone, phone, phone, phone,
Phone, phone, phone—
On the money-eating, outdoor, public phone!

See the housewife on the phone—
Kitchen phone!
Gabbing with a neighbor in a boring monotone!
Her poor husband's tried to reach her
That he's fired from his job,
That their daughter's socked her teacher,
And their son's a filthy creature
Who has joined up with the mob!
See him call, call, call,

But he has no luck at all!
For the line's tied up forever with the housewife's
Endless drone!
On the phone, phone, phone, phone,
Phone, phone, phone—
With the gabbing of the housewife on the phone!

See the bookie on the phone—
Private phone!
Taking bets on horses in his sleazy undertone!
See the fortune he has made off
All the suckers now in hock!
For the cops have all been paid off
And the Chief has called the raid off
That was set for three o'clock!
Making book, book, book,
Till the suckers all get took!
Making thousands from their wagers till their
Savings they have blown!
On the phone, phone, phone, phone,
Phone, phone, phone—
On the bookie's own unlisted private phone!

See the doctor on the phone—
Office phone!
Talking to a woman who is speaking in a moan!
She is feverish and aching
And she's lying on the floor!
But the doctor's head is shaking
As he tells her he's not making
Any house-calls anymore!
Hear her beg, beg, beg
That she's got a broken leg!
But the doctor kindly tells her that she's only
Bruised a bone!
On the phone, phone, phone, phone,

Phone, phone, phone!
On the doctor's ever-handy, off ice phone!

See the broker on the phone—
Wall Street phone!
Talking to investors in a confidential tone!
See how artfully he's told them
They should buy his gold-mine stock!
See the way that he's cajoled them
And the cunning way he's sold them
Each a whopping giant block!
How they'll swear, swear, swear
When they find the mine is bare—
And the broker's current whereabouts are
Suddenly unknown!
On the phone, phone, phone, phone.,
Phone, phone, phone—
When they find he's got a disconnected phone!

See the snooper on the phone—
Someone's phone!
Monitoring phone calls in his office all alone!
He can tap most any wire
That is linked to any spot!
And he always finds a buyer
Who is eager to acquire
What his dirty work has got!
How he'll grin, grin, grin
When he rakes the money in—
From the private talk of others that's no business
Of his own!
On the phone, phone, phone, phone,
Phone, phone, phone!
On some helpless victim's not-so-private phone!

30.

ANNABEL LEE

By Edgar Allan Poe

It was many and many a year ago,
    In a kingdom by the sea,
That a maiden there lived whom you may know
    By the name of Annabel Lee;
And this maiden she lived with no other thought
    Than to love and be loved by me.

I was a child and *she* was a child,
    In this kingdom by the sea:
But we loved with a love that was more than love—
    I and my Annabel Lee;
With a love that the winged seraphs of heaven
    Coveted her and me.

And this was the reason that, long ago,
    In this kingdom by the sea,
A wind blew out of a cloud, chilling
    My beautiful Annabel Lee;
So that her high-born kinsman came
    And bore her away from me,
To shut her up in a sepulchre
    In this kingdom by the sea.

The angels, not half so happy in heaven,
    Went envying her and me—

Yes!—that was the reason (as all men know,
    In this kingdom by the sea)
That the wind came out of the cloud by night,
    Chilling and killing my Annabel Lee.

But our love it was stronger by far than the love
    Of those who were older than we—
    Of many far wiser than we—
And neither the angels in heaven above,
    Nor the demons down under the sea,
Can ever dissever my soul from the soul
    Of the beautiful Annabel Lee.

For the moon never beams, without bringing me dreams
    Of the beautiful Annabel Lee;
And the stars never rise, but I feel the bright eyes
    Of the beautiful Annabel Lee;
And so, all the night-tide, I lie down by the side
Of my darling—my darling—my life and my bride,
    In the sepulchre there by the sea,
    In her tomb by the sounding sea.

CANNIBALEE

By Charles F. Lummis

It was many and many a year ago,
    On an island near the sea,
That a maiden lived whom you mightn't know
    By the name of Cannibalee;
And this maiden she lived with no other thought
    Than a passionate fondness for me.

I was a child, and *she* was a child—
    Tho' her tastes were adult Feejee—

But she loved with a love that was more than love,
 My yearning Cannibalee;
With a love that could take me roast or fried
 Or raw, as the case might be.

And that is the reason that long ago,
 In that island near the sea,
I had to turn the tables and eat
 My ardent Cannibalee—
Not really because I was fond of her,
 But to check her fondness for me.

But the stars never rise but I think of the size
 Of my hot-potted Cannibalee,
And the moon never stares but it brings me nightmares
 Of my spare-rib Cannibalee;
And all the night-tide she is restless inside,
Is my still indigestible dinner-belle bride,
In her pallid tomb, which is Me,
In her solemn sepulcher, Me.

THE CANNIBAL FLEA

By Tom Hood Jr.

It was many and many a year ago
 In a District called E. C.,
That a Monster dwelt whom I came to know
 By the name of Cannibal Flea,
And the brute was possessed with no other thought
 Than to live—and to live on me!

I was in bed, and *he* was in bed
 In the District named E. C.,
When first in his thirst so accurst he burst

Upon me, the Cannibal Flea,
    With a bite that felt as if some one had driven
A bayonet into me.

And this was the reason why long ago
    In that District named E. C.
I tumbled out of my bed, willing
    To capture the Cannibal Flea,
Who all the night until morning came
    Kept boring into me!
It wore me down to a skeleton
    In the District hight E. C.

From that hour I sought my bed—eleven—
    Till daylight he tortured me.
Yes!—that was the reason (as all men know
    In that District named E. C.)
I so often jumped out of my bed by night
    Willing the killing of Cannibal Flea.

But his hops they were longer by far than the hops
    Of creatures much larger than he—
Of parties more long-legged than he;
    And neither the powder nor turpentine drops,
Nor the persons engaged by me,
    Were so clever as ever to stop me the hop
Of the terrible Cannibal Flea.

For at night with a scream, I am waked from my dream
    By the terrible Cannibal Flea;
And at morn I ne'er rise without bites—of such size!—
    From the terrible Cannibal Flea.

So I'm forced to decide I'll no longer reside
    In the District—the District—where he doth abide,
The locality known as E. C.
    That is postally known as E. C.

SAMUEL BROWN

By Phoebe Cary

It was many and many a year ago,
    In a dwelling down in town,
That a fellow there lived whom you may know,
    By the name of Samuel Brown;
And this fellow he lived with no other thought
    Than to our house to come down.

I was a child, and *he* was a child,
    In that dwelling down in town,
But we loved with a love that was more than love,
    I and my Samuel Brown,—
With a love that the ladies coveted,
    Me and Samuel Brown.

And this was the reason that, long ago,
    To that dwelling down in town,
A girl came out of her carriage, courting
    My beautiful Samuel Brown;
So that her high-bred kinsmen came,
    And bore away Samuel Brown,
And shut him up in a dwelling house,
    In a street quite up in the town.

The ladies not half so happy up there,
    Went envying me and Brown;
Yes! that was the reason (as all men know,
    In this dwelling down in town),
That the girl came out of the carriage by night,
    Coquetting and getting my Samuel Brown.

But our love is more artful by far than the love
    Of those who are older than we,—

Of many far wiser than we,—
And neither the girls that are living above,
    Nor the girls that are down in town,
Can ever dissever my soul from the soul
    Of the beautiful Samuel Brown.

For the morn never shines, without bringing me lines,
    From my beautiful Samuel Brown
And the night 's never dark, but I sit in the park
    With my beautiful Samuel Brown.
And often by day, I walk down in Broadway,
With my darling, my darling, my life and my stay,
    To our dwelling down in town,
    To our house in the street down town.

ANNNABEL LEE

By Stanley Huntley

'Twas more than a million years ago,
    Or so it seems to me,
That I used to prance around and beau
    The beautiful Annabel Lee.
There were other girls in the neighborhood
    But none was a patch to she.

And this was the reason that long ago,
    My love fell out of a tree,
And busted herself on a cruel rock;
    A solemn sight to see,
For it spoiled the hat and gown and looks
    Of the beautiful Annabel Lee.

We loved with a love that was lovely love,
    I and my Annabel Lee,

And we went one day to gather the nuts
    That men call hickoree.
And I stayed below in the rosy glow
    While she shinned up the tree,
But no sooner up than down kerslup
    Came the beautiful Annabel Lee.

And the pallid moon and the hectic noon
    Bring gleams of dreams for me,
Of the desolate and desperate fate
    Of the beautiful Annabel Lee.
And I often think as I sink on the brink
Of slumber's sea, of the warm pink link
    That bound my soul to Annabel Lee;

And it wasn't just best for her interest
    To climb that hickory tree,
For had she stayed below with me,
    We'd had no hickory nuts maybe,
But I should have had my Annabel Lee.

31.

ULALUME

By Edgar Allan Poe

The skies they were ashen and sober;
　　The leaves they were crispéd and sere—
　　The leaves they were withering and sere:
It was night, in the lonesome October
　　Of my most immemorial year:
It was hard by the dim lake of Auber,
　　In the misty mid region of Weir—
It was down by the dank tarn of Auber,
　　In the ghoul-haunted woodland of Weir.

Here once, through an alley Titanic,
　　Of cypress, I roamed with my Soul—
　　Of cypress, with Psyche, my Soul.
These were days when my heart was volcanic
　　As the scoriac rivers that roll—
　　As the lavas that restlessly toll
Their sulphurous currents down Yaanek
　　In the ultimate climes of the Pole—
That groan as they roll down Mount Yaanek
　　In the realms of the Boreal Pole.

Our talk had been serious and sober ,
　　But our thoughts they were palsied and sere—
　　Our memories were treacherous and sere;
For we knew not the month was October,

And we marked not the night of the year
        (Ah, night of all nights in the year!)—
We noted not the dim lake of Auber
        (Though once we had journeyed down here)—
We remembered not the dank tarn of Auber,
        Nor the ghoul-haunted woodland of Weir.

And now, as the night was senescent
                And star-dials pointed to morn—
                As the star-dials hinted of morn—
At the end of our path a liquescent
        And nebulous lustre was born,
Out of which a miraculous crescent
        Arose with a duplicate horn—
Astarte's bediamonded crescent
        Distinct with its duplicate horn.

And I said: "She is warmer than Dian;
She rolls through an ether of sighs—
She revels in a region of sighs.
She has seen that the tears are not dry on
        These cheeks, where the worm never dies,
And has come past the stars of the Lion,
        To point us the path to the skies—
        To the Lethean peace of skies—
Come up, in despite of the Lion,
        To shine on us with her bright eyes—
Come up through the lair of the Lion,
With love in her luminous eyes."

But Psyche, uplifting her finger,
        Said: "Sadly this star I mistrust—
        Her pallor I strangely mistrust:
Ah, hasten!—ah, let us not linger!
        Ah, fly!—let us fly!—for we must."
In terror she spoke, letting sink her

Wings till they trailed in the dust—
In agony sobbed, letting sink her
 Plumes till they trailed in the dust—
 Till they sorrowfully trailed in the dust.

I replied: "This is nothing but dreaming:
Let us on by this tremulous light!
 Let us bathe in this crystalline light!
Its Sibyllic splendor is beaming
With Hope and in Beauty to-night:—
 See!—it flickers up the sky through the night!
Ah, we safely may trust to its gleaming,
 And be sure it will lead us aright—
We surely may trust to a gleaming,
That cannot but guide us aright,
Since it flickers up to Heaven through the night."

Thus I pacified Psyche and kissed her,
 And tempted her out of her gloom—
 And conquered her scruples and gloom;
And we passed to the end of the vista,
 But were stopped by the door of a tomb—
 By the door of a legended tomb;
And I said: "What is written, sweet sister,
 On the door of this legended tomb?"
 She replied: "Ulalume—Ulalume!—
'Tis the vault of thy lost Ulalume!"

Then my heart it grew ashen and sober
 As the leaves that were crispéd and sere—
 As the leaves that were withering and sere;
And I cried: "It was surely October
 On *this* very night of last year
 That I journeyed—I journeyed down here!—
 That I brought a dread burden down here—
 On this night of all nights in the year,
 Ah, what demon hath tempted me here?

Well I know, now, this dim lake of Auber—
    This misty mid region of Weir—
Well I know, now, this dank tarn of Auber,
    This ghoul-haunted woodland of Weir."

Said we, then—the two, then: "Ah, can it
    Have been that the woodlandish ghouls—
    The pitiful, the merciful ghouls—
To bar up our way and to ban it
    From the secret that lies in these wolds—
    From the thing that lies hidden in these wolds—
Have drawn up the spectre of a planet
    From the limbo of lunary souls—
This sinfully scintillant planet
    From the Hell of the planetary souls?"

The Willows

By Bret Harte

The skies they were ashen and sober,
    The streets they were dirty and drear;
It was night in the month of October,
    Of my most immemorial year.
Like the skies, I was perfectly sober,
    As I stopped at the mansion of Shear,—
At the Nightingale,—perfectly sober,
    And the willowy woodland down here.

Here, once in an alley Titanic
    Of Ten-pins, I roamed with my soul,—
    Of Ten-pins, with Mary, my soul;
They were days when my heart was volcanic
    And impelled me to frequently roll,
    And made me resistlessly roll,

Till my ten-strikes created a panic
    In the realms of the Boreal pole,—
Till my ten-strikes created a panic
    With the monkey atop of his pole.

I repeat, I was perfectly sober,
    But my thoughts they were palsied and sear,—
    My thoughts were decidedly queer;
For I knew not the month was October,
    And I marked not the night of the year;
I forgot that sweet *morceau* of Auber
    That the band oft performèd down here, -
And I mixed the sweet music of Auber
    With the Nightingale's music by Shear.

And now as the night was senescent,
    And star-dials pointed to morn,
    And car-drivers hinted of morn,
At the end of the path a liquescent
    And bibulous lustre was born;
't was made by the bar-keeper present,
    Who mixèd a duplicate horn,—
His two hands describing a crescent
    Distinct with a duplicate horn.

And I said: "This looks perfectly regal,
    For it's warm, and I know I feel dry,—
    I am confident that I feel dry.
We have come past the emeu and eagle,
    And watched the gay monkey on high;
Let us drink to the emeu and eagle,
    To the swan and the monkey on high,—
    To the eagle and monkey on high;
For this bar-keeper will not inveigle,
    Bully boy with the vitreous eye,—
He surely would never inveigle,
    Sweet youth with the crystalline eye."

But Mary, uplifting her finger,
 Said: "Sadly this bar I mistrust,—
 I fear that this bar does not trust.
Oh, hasten! oh, let us not linger!
 Oh, fly—let us fly,—ere we must!"
In terror she cried, letting sink her
 Parasol till it trailed in the dust;
In agony sobbed, letting sink her
 Parasol till it trailed in the dust,—
 Till it sorrowfully trailed in the dust.

Then I pacified Mary and kissed her,
 And tempted her into the room,
 And conquered her scruples and gloom;
And we passed to the end of the vista,
 But were stopped by the warning of doom,—
 By some words that were warning of doom.
And I said, "What is written, sweet sister,
 At the opposite end of the room?"
She sobbed, as she answered, "All liquors
 Must be paid for ere leaving the room."

Then my heart it grew ashen and sober,
 As the streets were deserted and drear,
 For my pockets were empty and drear;
And I cried : "It was surely October,
 On this very night of last year,
 That I journeyed, I journeyed down here,—
 That I brought a fair maiden down here,
 On this night of all nights in the year!
 Ah! to me that inscription is clear;
Well I know now, I'm perfectly sober,
 Why no longer they credit me here,—
Well I know now that music of Auber,
 And this Nightingale, kept by one Shear."

32.

THE RAVEN

By Edgar Allan Poe

Once upon a midnight dreary, while I pondered, weak and
    weary,
Over many a quaint and curious volume of forgotten lore—
While I nodded, nearly napping, suddenly there came a
    tapping,
As of some one gently rapping, rapping at my chamber door.
"'Tis some visitor," I muttered, "tapping at my chamber
    door—
        Only this and nothing more."

Ah, distinctly I remember it was in the bleak December;
And each separate dying ember wrought its ghost upon the
    floor.
Eagerly I wished the morrow;—vainly I had sought to borrow
From my books surcease of sorrow—sorrow for the lost Lenore—
For the rare and radiant maiden whom the angels name
    Lenore—
        Nameless *here* for evermore.

And the silken, sad, uncertain rustling of each purple curtain
Thrilled me—filled me with fantastic terrors never felt before;
So that now, to still the beating of my heart, I stood repeating
"'Tis some visitor entreating entrance at my chamber door—
Some late visitor entreating entrance at my chamber door;—
        This it is and nothing more."

Presently my soul grew stronger; hesitating then no longer,
"Sir," said I, "or Madam, truly your forgiveness I implore;
But the fact is I was napping, and so gently you came rapping,
And so faintly you came tapping, tapping at my chamber
    door,
That I scarce was sure I heard you"—here I opened wide the
    door;—
        Darkness there and nothing more.

Deep into that darkness peering, long I stood there
    wondering, fearing,
Doubtful, dreaming dreams no mortal ever dared to dream
    before;
But the silence was unbroken, and the stillness gave no token,
And the only word there spoken was the whispered word,
    "Lenore!"
This I whispered, and an echo murmured back the word
    "Lenore!"
Merely this and nothing more.

Back into the chamber turning, all my soul within me
    burning,
Soon again I heard a tapping somewhat louder than before.
"Surely," said I, "surely that is something at my window
    lattice;
Let me see, then, what thereat is, and this mystery explore—
Let my heart be still a moment and this mystery explore;—
        'Tis the wind and nothing more!"

Open here I flung the shutter, when, with many a flirt and
    flutter,
In there stepped a stately Raven of the saintly days of yore.
Not the least obeisance made he; not a minute stopped or
    stayed he;
But, with mien of lord or lady, perched above my chamber
    door—

Perched upon a bust of Pallas just above my chamber door—
    Perched, and sat, and nothing more.

Then this ebony bird beguiling my sad fancy into smiling,
By the grave and stern decorum of the countenance it wore,
"Though thy crest be shorn and shaven, thou," I said, "art
    sure no craven,
Ghastly grim and ancient Raven wandering from the Nightly
    shore—
Tell me what thy lordly name is on the Night's Plutonian
    shore!"
    Quoth the Raven, "Nevermore."

Much I marvelled this ungainly fowl to hear discourse so
    plainly,
Though its answer little meaning—little relevancy bore;
For we cannot help agreeing that no living human being
Ever yet was blessed with seeing bird above his chamber
    door—
Bird or beast upon the sculptured bust above his chamber door,
With such name as "Nevermore."

But the Raven, sitting lonely on the placid bust, spoke only
That one word, as if his soul in that one word he did outpour.
Nothing farther then he uttered-not a feather then he
    fluttered—
Till I scarcely more than muttered "Other friends have flown
    before—
On the morrow *he* will leave me, as my hopes have flown
    before."
    Then the bird said "Nevermore."

Startled at the stillness broken by reply so aptly spoken,
"Doubtless," said I, "what it utters is its only stock and store
Caught from some unhappy master whom unmerciful
    Disaster

Followed fast and followed faster till his songs one burden
    bore—
Till the dirges of his Hope that melancholy burden bore
        Of 'Never—nevermore.' "

But the Raven still beguiling all my fancy into smiling,
Straight I wheeled a cushioned seat in front of bird, and bust
    and door;
Then, upon the velvet sinking, I betook myself to linking
Fancy unto fancy, thinking what this ominous bird of yore—
What this grim, ungainly, ghastly, gaunt, and ominous bird of
    yore
Meant in croaking "Nevermore."

This I sat engaged in guessing, but no syllable expressing
To the fowl whose fiery eyes now burned into my bosom's
    core;
This and more I sat divining, with my head at ease reclining
On the cushion's velvet lining that the lamp-light gloated
    o'er,
But whose velvet violet lining with the lamp-light gloating
    o'er,
        She shall press, ah, nevermore!

Then, methought, the air grew denser, perfumed from an
    unseen censer
Swung by Seraphim whose foot-falls tinkled on the tufted
    floor.
"Wretch," I cried, "thy God hath lent thee—by these angels
    he hath sent thee
Respite—respite and nepenthe from thy memories of Lenore;
Quaff, oh quaff this kind nepenthe and forget this lost
    Lenore!"
        Quoth the Raven, "Nevermore."

"Prophet!" said I, "thing of evil!—prophet still, if bird or
    devil!—

Whether Tempter sent, or whether tempest tossed thee here
    ashore,
Desolate yet all undaunted, on this desert land enchanted—
On this home by Horror haunted—tell me truly, I implore—
Is there—*is* there balm in Gilead?—tell me—tell me, I
    implore!"
        Quoth the Raven "Nevermore."

"Prophet!" said I, "thing of evil—prophet still, if bird or devil!
By that Heaven that bends above us—by that God we both
    adore—
Tell this soul with sorrow laden if, within the distant Aidenn,
It shall clasp a sainted maiden whom the angels name
    Lenore—
Clasp a rare and radiant maiden whom the angels name
    Lenore."
        Quoth the Raven "Nevermore."

"Be that word our sign of parting, bird or fiend!" I shrieked,
    upstarting—
"Get thee back into the tempest and the Night's Plutonian
    shore!
Leave no black plume as a token of that lie thy soul hath
    spoken!
Leave my loneliness unbroken!—quit the bust above my
    door!
Take thy beak from out my heart, and take thy form from off
    my door!"
        Quoth the Raven "Nevermore."

And the Raven, never flitting, still is sitting, *still* is sitting
On the pallid bust of Pallas just above my chamber door;
And his eyes have all the seeming of a demon's that is
    dreaming,
And the lamp-light o'er him streaming throws his shadow on
    the floor;

And my soul from out that shadow that lies floating on the
  floor
        Shall be lifted—nevermore!

Mysterious Rappings

By Benjamin Penhallow Shillaber

Late one evening I was sitting, gloomy shadows round me
    flitting,—
Mrs. Partington, a-knitting, occupied the grate before;
Suddenly I heard a patter, a slight and very trifling matter,
As if it were a thieving rat or mouse within my closet door;
A thieving and mischievous rat or mouse within my closet
door,—
        Only this, and nothing more.

Then all my dreaminess forsook me; rising up I straightway,
    shook me,
A light from off the table took, and swift the rat's destruction
    swore,
Mrs. P. smiled approbation on my prompt determination,
And without more hesitation oped I wide the closet door;
Boldly, without hesitation, opened wide the closet door;
        Darkness there, and nothing more!

As up on the sound I pondered, what the deuce it was I
    wondered;
Could it be my ear had blundered, as at times it had before?
But scarce again was I reseated, ere I heard the sound
    repeated,
The same dull patter that had greeted me from out the closet
    door;
Heard the patter that bad greeted me from out the closet door;
        A gentle patter, nothing more.

Then my rage arose unbounded—"What," cried I, "is this
   confounded
Noise with which my ear is wounded—noise I've never heard
   before?
If 'tis presage dread of evil, if 'tis made by ghost or devil,
I call on ye to be more civil—'stop that knocking at the door!'
Stop that strange, mysterious knocking, there within my
   closet door;
      Grant me this, if nothing more."

Once again I seized the candle, rudely grasped the latchet's
   handle,
Savage its a Goth or Vandal, that kicked up rumpuses of
   yore—
What the dickens is the matter," said I, " to produce this
   patter?"
To Mrs. P., and looked straight at her. "I don't know," said
   she, "I'm shore;
Lest it be a pesky rat; or something, I don't know, I'm shore."
      This she said, and nothing more.

Still the noise kept on unceasing; evidently 'twas increasing;
Like a cart-wheel wanting greasing, wore it on my nerves full
   sore;
Patter, patter, patter, patter! the rain the while made noisy
   clatter,
My teeth with boding ill did chatter, as when I'm troubled by
   a bore—
Some prosing, dull, and dismal fellow, coming in but just to
   bore—
      Only this, and nothing more.

All night long it kept on tapping; vain I laid myself for
   mapping,
Calling sleep ray sense to wrap in darkness till the night was
   o'er;

A dismal candle, dimly burning, watched me as I lay there
    turning,
In desperation wildly yearning that sleep would visit me
    once more;
Sleep, refreshing sleep, did I most urgently implore;
        This I wished, and nothing more.

With the day I rose next morning, and, all idle terror scorning
Went to finding out the warning that annoyed me so before;
When straightway, to my consternation, daylight made the
    revelation
Of a scene of devastation that annoyed me very sore,
Such a scene of devastation as annoyed me very sore.
        This it was, and nothing more:—

The rotten roof had taken leaking, and the rain, a passage
    seeking,
Through the murky darkness sneaking, found my hat-box on
    the floor:
There, exposed to dire disaster, lay my brand-new Sunday
    castor.
And its hapless, luckless master ne'er shall see its beauties
    more—
Ne'er shall see its glossy beauty, that his glory was before;
        It is gone, for evermore!

POE'S RAVEN

By Joseph Bert Smiley, from
Local and National Poets of America
(American Publishers' Association, 1890)

How distinctly I remember, late one evening last, November,
I was sitting on a barrel that the moonlight gloated o'er—
'Twas an empty elder barrel and was useful now no more—
        Worthless, now, forevermore.

As a few lone stars were blinking, I betook myself to
    thinking,
And I thought of that old raven Edgar Poe has told about—
That was quite a high old raven Mr. Poe has told about.
I kept thinking, thinking, thinking, as those stars kept
    blinking, blinking,
And the more I thought about it, I was more and more in
    doubt;
        Edgar's logic knocked me out.

And I found no explanation to that curious situation—
Here's the lamp upon the table, and the raven on the door,
And the lamplight o'er him streaming throw his shadow on
    the floor.
Think of where the lamp was sitting and you cannot help
    admitting
'Twas an awful crooked shadow to have ever reached the
    floor.
'Twas a hump-backed, cross-eyed shadow if it ever saw the
    floor.
So I sought a clear solution to that shadow's dire confusion,
And my only strong conclusion wits that Edgar had the
    snakes.
I am sure he had been drinking and he must have had the
    studies.
So perhaps the raven, sitting on the cornice, never flitting,
With its fiery eyes it burning into Edgar's bosom core
Was the whisky he'd been drinking just before he fell to
    thinking
Of his lovely lost Lenore.
        It was bug-juice, evermore.

Or perhaps the maiden, deeming she a fellow too demeaning,
Had preferred to share the fortunes of the friends who'd gone
    before,
And had perished, broken-hearted, as fair maids have done
    before.

Maybe he disgraced and slighted till she felt her life was
    blighted
And her lonely soul, benighted, wandered to a fairer shore,
Maybe Edgar's drinking killed her, as it has killed girls
    before.
        It was benzine, evermore.

Get most anybody frisky on a quart or two of whiskey
And he'd think he saw some shadows, or some ravens, or
    some floors,
And the lamps would got befuddled and the shadows awful
    muddled,
And he'd see one crazy raven perched on forty-'leven doors;
And he wouldn't know a shutter from a a dozen lost Lenores.
It is my profound opinion that if Poe had kept dominion
O'er his brains and o'or his reason, as they used to be of
    yore—
That if he had been less frisky and had guzzled down less
    whiskey
He'd have never been that raven on the trust above his door.
Very likely that same evening he'd been on a bust before.
        And got sober—nevermore.

THE GOBLIN GOOSE

Carolyn Wells, in her Parody Anthology, *credits this poem to*
"Punch," no author, no date.

Once it happened I'd been dining, on my couch I slept
    reclining,
And awoke with moonlight shining brightly on my bedroom
    floor,
It was in the bleak December, Christmas night as I remember,
But I had no dying ember, as Poe had, when near the door,
Like a gastronomic goblin just beside my chamber door
        Stood a bird,—and nothing more.

And I said, for I 'm no craven, "Are you Edgar's famous
    raven,
Seeking as with him a haven—were you mixed up with
    Lenore?"
Then the bird uprose and fluttered, and this sentence strange
    he uttered,
"Hang Lenore," he mildly muttered; "you have seen me once
    before,
Seen me on this festive Christmas, seen me surely once
    before,
        I'm the Goose—and nothing more."

Then he murmured, "Are you ready?" and with motion slow
    and steady,
Straight he leapt upon my bed; he simply gave a stifled roar;
And I cried, "As I'm a sinner, at a Goose-Club I was winner,
'T is a memory of my dinner, which I ate at halfpast four,
Goose well-stuffed with sage and onions, which I ate at half-
    past four."
        Quoth he hoarsely, "Eat no more!"

Said I, "I've enjoyed your juices, breast and back; but tell me,
    Goose, is
This revenge, and what the use is of your being such a bore?
For Goose-flesh I will no more ax, if you 'll not sit on my
    thorax,
Go try honey mixed with borax, for I hear your throat is sore,
You speak gruffly, though too plainly, and I 'm sure your
    throat is sore."
        Quoth the nightmare, "Eat no more!"

"Goose!" I shrieked out, "leave, oh, leave me, surely you
    don't mean to grieve me,
You are heavy, pray reprieve me, now my penance must be
    o'er;
Though to-night you've brought me sorrow, comfort surely
    comes to-morrow,

Some relief from those I'd borrow at my doctor's ample
    store."
        Quoth the goblin, "Eat no more!"

And that fat Goose, never flitting, like a nightmare still is
    sitting
With me all the night emitting words that thrill my bosom's
    core,
Now throughout the Christmas season, while I lie and gasp
    and wheeze, on
Me he sits until my reason nothing surely can restore,
       While that Goose says, "Eat no more!"

33.

THE LOST CHORD

By Adelaide Ann Proctor

Seated one day at the Organ,
    I was weary and ill at ease,
And my fingers wandered idly
    Over the noisy keys.

I do not know what I was playing,
    Or what I was dreaming then;
But I struck one chord of music,
    Like the sound of a great Amen.

It flooded the crimson twilight,
    Like the close of an Angel's Psalm,
And it lay on my fevered spirit
    With a touch of infinite calm.

It quieted pain and sorrow,
    Like love overcoming strife;
It seemed the harmonious echo
    From our discordant life.

It linked all perplexèd meanings
    Into one perfect peace,
And trembled away into silence
    As if it were loth to cease.

Adelaide Ann Proctor

I have sought, but I seek it vainly,
    That one lost chord divine,
Which came from the soul of the Organ,
    And entered into mine.

It may be that Death's bright angel
    Will speak in that chord again,—
It may be that only in Heaven
    I shall hear that grand Amen.

THE LOST WORD

By John Paul, pseudonym of Charles Henry Webb.

Seated one day at the typewriter,
    I was weary of a's and e's,
And my fingers wandered wildly
    Over the consonant keys.

I know not what I was writing,
    With that thing so like a pen;
But I struck one word astounding—
    Unknown to the speech of men.

It flooded the sense of my verses,
    Like the break of a tinker's dam,
And I felt as one feels when the printer
    Of your "infinite calm" makes clam.

It mixed up s's and x's
    Like an alphabet coming to strife.
It seemed the discordant echo
    Of a row between husband and wife.

It brought a perplexed meaning
    Into my perfect piece,
And set the machinery creaking
    As though it were scant of grease.

I have tried, but I try it vainly,
   The one last word to divine
Which came from the keys of my typewriter
   And so would pass as mine.

It may be some other typewriter
   Will produce that word again,
It may be, but only for others—
   I shall write henceforth with a pen.

THE FOUND CHORD

By Franklin P. Adams, from So There! (Doubleday Page, 1923)

Standing one day at the saxophone,
   I was peppy and full of booze,
And my fingers wandered madly
   Playing "The Blah Blah Blues."

I knew just what I was playing,
   And what I had swiped it from;
And I stole one strain of music
   And I said to myself, "Ho! hum!"

I stole six bars from Wagner,
   Seven from Rubinstein;
And I said, "I'll bet I can sell this
   Melody that is mine."

And a music publisher heard it
   And said, in a way he has:
"I'll tell the world you've got a hit;
   Oh kid, that is some jazz."

And the thing sold in the millions,
    And brought me wealth and fame;
And the blush of pride was on my cheek,
    But never the blush of shame.

It may be that Richard Wagner,
    And Anton von Rubinstein
Are turning in their graves now,
    But the royalties are mine.

34.

FOG

By Carl Sandburg

The fog comes
on little cat feet.
It sits looking
over harbor and city
on silent haunches
and then moves on.

ROAD FOG

By Armand T. Ringer

The fog comes
on little cat feet.
It blankets
the Blue Ridge Parkway,
hiding the beautiful
mountains and valleys
of North Carolina.
I crawl cautiously
along the road
at ten miles an hour,
cursing that blasted
cat for not moving on.

35.

The Shooting of Dan McGrew

By Robert Service

A bunch of the boys were whooping it up in the Malamute
    saloon;
The kid that handles the music-box was hitting a jag-time
    tune;
Back of the bar, in a solo game, sat Dangerous Dan McGrew,
And watching his luck was his light-o'-love, the lady that's
    known as Lou.

When out of the night, which was fifty below, and into the
    din and the glare,
There stumbled a miner fresh from the creeks, dog-dirty, and
    loaded for bear.
He looked like a man with a foot in the grave and scarcely the
    strength of a louse,
Yet he tilted a poke of dust on the bar, and he called for
    drinks for the house.
There was none could place the stranger's face, though we
    searched ourselves for a clue,
But we drank his health, and the last to drink was Dangerous
    Dan McGrew.

There's men that somehow just grip your eyes, and hold
    them hard like a spell;
And such was he, and he looked to me like a man who had
    lived in hell;

With a face most hair, and the dreary stare of a dog whose
    day is done,
As he watered the green stuff in his glass, and the drops fell
    one by one.
Then I got to figgering who he was, and wondering what
    he'd do,
And I turned my head-and there watching him was the lady
    that's known as Lou.

His eyes went rubbering round the room, and he seemed in a
    kind of daze,
Till at last that old piano fell in the way of his wandering gaze.
The rag-time kid was having a drink; there was no one else
    on the stool,
So the stranger stumbles across the room, and flops down
    there like a fool.
In a buckskin shirt that was glazed with dirt he sat, and I saw
    him sway;
Then he clutched the keys with his talon hands—my God! but
    that man could play.

Were you ever out in the Great Alone, when the moon was
    awful clear,
And the icy mountains hemmed you in with a silence you
    could almost hear;
With only the howl of a timber wolf, and you camped there
    in the cold,
A half-dead thing in a stark, dead world, clean mad for the
    muck called gold;
While high overhead, green, yellow and red, the North Lights
    swept in bars?
Then you've a hunch what the music meant . . . hunger and
    night and the stars.

And hunger not of the belly kind, that's banished with bacon
    and beans,

But the gnawing hunger of lonely men for a home and all
    that it means;
For a fireside far from the cares that are, four walls and a roof
    above;
But oh! so cramful of cosy joy, and crowned with a woman's
    love—
A woman dearer than all the world, and true as Heaven is
    true—
(God! how ghastly she looks through her rouge,—the lady
    that's known as Lou.)

Then on a sudden the music changed, so soft that you scarce
    could hear;
But you felt that your life had been looted clean of all that it
    once held dear;
That someone had stolen the woman you loved; that her love
    was a devil's lie;
That your guts were gone, and the best for you was to crawl
    away and die.
'Twas the crowning cry of a heart's despair, and it thrilled
    you through and through—
"I guess I'll make it a spread misère," said Dangerous Dan
    McGrew.

The music almost died away . . . then it burst like a pent-up
    flood;
And it seemed to say, "Repay, repay," and my eyes were blind
    with blood.
The thought came back of an ancient wrong, and it stung like
    a frozen lash,
And the lust awoke to kill, to kill . . . then the music stopped
    with a crash,
And the stranger turned, and his eyes they burned in a most
    peculiar way;
In a buckskin shirt that was glazed with dirt he sat, and I saw
    him sway;

Then his lips went in in a kind of grin, and he spoke, and his
  voice was calm,
And "Boys," says he, "you don't know me, and none of you
  care a damn;
But I want to state, and my words are straight, and I'll bet my
  poke they're true,
That one of you is a hound of hell . . . and that one is Dan
  McGrew."

Then I ducked my head, and the lights went out, and two
  guns blazed in the dark,
And a woman screamed, and the lights went up, and two
  men lay stiff and stark.
Pitched on his head, and pumped full of lead, was Dangerous
  Dan McGrew,
While the man from the creeks lay clutched to the breast of
  the lady that's known as Lou.

These are the simple facts of the case, and I guess I ought to
  know.
They say that the stranger was crazed with "hooch," and I'm
  not denying it's so.
I'm not so wise as the lawyer guys, but strictly between us
  two—
The woman that kissed him and—pinched his poke—was the
  lady that's known as Lou.

THE SHOOTING OF DAN McGINK

*This parody of Robert Service's most famous poem was sent to me by
Elizabeth E. Erickson, of Phoenix, Arizona. She had memorized the
poem when she was ten, and wrote it down from memory. She did not
recall the poet's name, but thinks that the poem was in a humor
column which appeared now and then in the* Detroit Times.

A bunch of the boys were whooping it up in the Milk and
     Water Saloon,
And the kid that peddled the lollypops was licking the ice
     cream spoon.
A-reading a tract in a whiny voice sat Dangerous Dan
     McGink,
And at his side sat his blushing bride, a vision in mauve and
     pink.

When out of the snow that filled Park Row, and into the
     lighted room,
There burst a bird by the name of Furd, with a voice like the
     crack of doom.
A bearded bird by the name of Furd, and he held us with his
     stare.
And now and again, he waxed profane—-My goodness! how
     he could swear!

"You boys," said he, "you don't know me, and I guess I don't
     know you,
But I've sallied forth from the frozen North to sip a soda or
     two."
Then, spying a piano near the door, there he made his way,
He began to pound the keys around—-My goodness! how he
     could play!

We all joined in, and the chorus swelled, and we sang ten
     hymns or so,
But the voice of McGink was the worst, I think, as it echoed
     high and low.
Then up spoke that bird by the name of Furd, "Desist! Desist!
     Desist!"
And seizing a peashooter from the bar he shot McGink in the
     wrist!

Oh, the boys were whooping it up that night, in the Milk and
    Water Saloon,
And the kid that peddled the lollypops was licking the ice
    cream spoon,
Now, I've written a lot of terrible rot, but never did I think
I would live to write of that awful night, of the shooting of
    Dan McGink!

36.

OZYMANIAS

By Percy Bysshe Shelley

I met a traveller from an antique land
Who said: Two vast and trunkless legs of stone
Stand in the desert . . . Near them, on the sand,
Half sunk, a shattered visage lies, whose frown,
And wrinkled lip, and sneer of cold command,
Tell that its sculptor well those passions read
Which yet survive, stamped on these lifeless things,
The hand that mocked them, and the heart that fed:
And on the pedestal these words appear:
"My name is Ozymandias, king of kings:
Look on my works, ye Mighty, and despair!"
Nothing beside remains. Round the decay
Of that colossal wreck, boundless and bare
The lone and level sands stretch far away.

OZYMANDIAS REVISITED

By Morris Bishop, from Paramount Poems (1929)

I met a traveller from an antique land
Who said: Two vast and trunkless legs of stone
Stand in the desert . . . Near them on the sand,
Half sunk, a shatter'd visage lies, whose frown
And wrinkled lip and sneer of cold command

Tell that its sculptor well those passions read
Which yet survive, stamp'd on these lifeless things,
The hand that mocked them and the heart that fed;
And on the pedestal these words appear:
"My name is Ozymandias, king of kings!
Look on my works, ye Mighty, and despair!"
Also the names of Emory P. Gray,
Mr. and Mrs. Dukes, and Oscar Baer,
Of 17 West 4th Street, Oyster Bay.

37.

THE BATTLE OF BLENHEIM

By Robert Southey

It was a summer evening,
    Old Kaspar's work was done,
And he before his cottage door
    Was sitting in the Sun,
And by him sported on the green
His little grandchild Wilhelmine.

She saw her brother Peterkin
    Roll something large and round,
Which he beside the rivulet
    In playing there had found;
He came to ask what he had found,
That was so large, and smooth, and round.

Old Kaspar took it from the boy,
    Who stood expectant by;
And then the old man shook his head,
    And with a natural sigh,
" 'Tis some poor fellow's skull," said he,
"Who fell in the great victory.

"I find them in the garden,
    For there's many here about;
And often when I go to plough,
    The ploughshare turns them out!

171

For many thousand men," said he,
"Were slain in that great victory."

"Now tell us what 't was all about,"
     Young Peterkin, he cries;
And little Wilhelmine looks up
     With wonder-waiting eyes;
"Now tell us all about the war,
And what they fought each other for."

"It was the English," Kaspar cried,
     "Who put the French to rout;
But what they fought each other for,
     I could not well make out;
But every body said," quoth he,
"That 't was a famous victory.

"My father lived at Blenheim then,
     Yon little stream hard by;
They burnt his dwelling to the ground,
     And he was forced to fly;
So with his wife and child he fled,
Nor had he where to rest his head.

"With fire and sword the country round
     Was wasted far and wide,
And many a childing mother then,
     And new-born baby died;
But things like that, you know, must be
At every famous victory.

"They say it was a shocking sight
     After the field was won;
For many thousand bodies here
     Lay rotting in the Sun;
But things like that, you know, must be
After a famous victory.

"Great praise the Duke of Marlbro' won,
    And our good Prince Eugene."
"Why 't was a very wicked thing!"
    Said little Wilhelmine.
"Nay . . . nay . . . my little girl," quoth he.
"It was a famous victory.

"And everybody praised the Duke
    Who this great fight did win."
"But what good came of it at last?"
    Quoth little Peterkin.
"Why that I cannot tell," said he,
"But 't was a famous victory."

IT WAS A FAMOUS VICTORY

By Franklin P. Adams, in Something Else Again *(1920)*

It was a summer evening;
    Old Kaspar was at home,
Sitting before his cottage door—
    Like in the Southey pome—
And near him, with a magazine,
Idled his grandchild, Geraldine.

"Why don't you ask me," Kaspar said
    To the child upon the floor,
"Why don't you ask me what I did
    When I was in the war?
They told me that each little kid
Would surely ask me what I did.

"I've had my story ready
    For thirty years or more."
"Don't bother, Grandpa," said the child;

"I find such things a bore.
Pray leave me to my magazine,"
Asserted little Geraldine.

Then entered little Peterkin,
    To whom his gaffer said:
"You'd like to hear about the war?
    How I was left for dead?"
"No. And, besides," declared the youth,
"How do I know you speak the truth?"

Arose that wan, embittered man,
    The hero of this pome,
And walked, with not unsprightly step,
    Down to the Soldiers' Home,
Where he, with seven other men,
Sat swapping lies till half-past ten.

38.

HAPPY THOUGHT

By Robert Louis Stevenson

The world is so full of a number of things,
I'm sure we should all be as happy as kings.

FUNNY THOUGHT

By Franklin P. Adams, in Something Else Again (1920).

This town is so full of a number of folks,
I'm sure there will always be matter for jokes.

FURTHER THOUGHTS

by Armand T. Ringer.

Whimsical Thought

> The world is still full of a number of kings,
> And thousands of other ridiculous things.

Deep Thought

> The sky is so full of a number of stars,
> I'm sure there are millions of planets like ours.

Prayerful Thought

> The world is so full of violence and sleaze,
> We should all bow our heads and get down on our knees.

Finnegan Thought

> The word is so fool of a numble of thinks,
> Siam shore we sud oil be as hippy as kinks.

Political Thought

> D.C. is so full of political hacks,
> I'm amazed that our country still runs on its tracks.

Freudian Thought

> The world still is full of admirers of Freud.
> Don't call him a quack! They'll be very annoyed!

Art Thought

> SoHo is so full of preposterous art,
> That I'd rather go look at a tree in the park.

Reptilian Thought

> The world is so full of a number of snakes,
> Just thinking about it now gives me the shakes.

Poetical Thought

> The *New Yorker* prints such unmusical verse,
> I am sure that its poetry couldn't be worse.

Economic Thought

> The market's so full of stock values that rise,
> We should all be prepared for a sudden surprise.

Environmental Thought

> The world is so full of birth rates exploding,
> I am sure there are precious resources eroding.

Theological Thought

> The world is so full of things that appall,
> I wonder if God is aware of it all.

Educational Thought

> Our schools are so full of incompetent teachers,
> They may even outnumber fundamentalist preachers.

Terminal Thought

> Writing such verse is beginning to bore,
> I hope that my readers will send us some more.

39.

The Star

By Jane Taylor

Twinkle, twinkle, little star,
How I wonder what you are
Up above the world so high,
Like a diamond in the sky.
Twinkle, twinkle, little star,
How I wonder what you are.

When the blazing Sun is gone,
When he nothing shines upon,
Then you show your little light,
Twinkle, twinkle, all the night.
Twinkle, twinkle, little star,
How I wonder what you are.

Then the traveller in the dark
Thanks you for your tiny spark,
He could not see where to go
If you did not twinkle so.
Twinkle, twinkle, little star,
How I wonder what you are.

In the dark blue sky you keep,
While you through my curtains peep,
And you never shut your eye
Till the Sun is in the sky.

Twinkle, twinkle, little star,
How I wonder what you are.

TWINKLE, LITTLE CAR

By Dave Morice

Twinkle, twinkle, little car,
How I wonder what you are.
From this distance, who could say
Cadillac or Chevrolet?

Twinkle, twinkle, little car,
How I wonder what you are
In the distance shining bright.
I'll never know. You just turned right.

TWINKLE, LITTLE STAR

By Armand T. Ringer

Twinkle, twinkle, little star,
I know *exactly* what you are.
You're just a sun. How do I know?
My science teacher told me so.

TO SHIRLEY TEMPLE

By Armand T. Ringer

Twinkle, twinkle, little star,
I wonder just how old you are.
You look as if you're only five.
Are you a midget in disguise?

40.

CROSSING THE BAR

By Alfred, Lord Tennyson

Sunset and evening star,
    And one clear call for me!
And may there be no moaning of the bar,
    When I put out to sea,

But such a tide as moving seems asleep,
    Too full for sound and foam,
When that which drew from out the boundless deep
    Turns again home.

Twilight and evening bell,
    And after that the dark!
And may there be no sadness of farewell,
    When I embark;

For tho' from out our bourne of Time and Place
    The flood may bear me far,
I hope to see my Pilot face to face
    When I have crost the bar.

Alfred, Lord Tennyson

LEAVING THE BAR

By Alfred Lord Tennis Shoes
(pseudonym of Armand T. Ringer)

Sunset and evening star,
    My wife will furious be,
And may there be no moaning at the bar
    When I decide to flee.

The patrons of the house are half asleep,
    Too full of beer and foam,
I pay the tab—the rye's not cheap!—
    Then I embark for home.

For tho' from out this smoke filled room
  A cab may bear me far,
I soon will see my angry spouse's face
  When I have left the bar.

41.

BEAUTIFUL SNOW

By John Whitaker Watson

Oh! the snow, the beautiful snow,
Filling the sky and the earth below;
Over the house-tops, over the street,
Over the heads of the people you meet;
       Dancing,
          Flirting,
             Skimming along.
Beautiful snow! it can do nothing wrong.
Flying to kiss a fair lady's cheek;
Clinging to lips in a frolicsome freak.
Beautiful snow, from the heavens above,
Pure as an angel and fickle as love!

Oh! the snow, the beautiful snow!
How the flakes gather and laugh as they go!
Whirling about in its maddening fun,
It plays in its glee with every one.
       Chasing,
          Laughing,
             Hurrying by,
It lights up the face and it sparkles the eye;
And even the dogs, with a bark and a bound,
Snap at the crystals that eddy around.
The town is alive, and its heart in a glow
To welcome the coming of beautiful snow.

185

How the wild crowd goes swaying along,
Hailing each other with humor and song!
How the gay sledges like meteors flash by—
Bright for a moment, then lost to the eye.
      Ringing,
        Swinging,
          Dashing they go
Over the crest of the beautiful snow:
Snow so pure when it falls from the sky,
To be trampled in mud by the crowd rushing by;
To be trampled and tracked by the thousands of feet
Till it blends with the horrible filth in the street.

Once I was pure as the snow—but I fell:
Fell, like the snow-flakes, from heaven-to hell:
Fell, to be tramped as the filth of the street:
Fell, to be scoffed, to be spit on and beat.
      Pleading,
        Cursing,
          Dreading to die,
Selling my soul to whoever would buy,
Dealing in shame for a morsel of bread,
Hating the living and fearing the dead.
Merciful God! have I fallen so low?
And yet I was once like this beautiful snow!

Once I was fair as the beautiful snow,
With an eye like its crystals, a heart like its glow;
Once I was loved for my innocent grace—
Flattered and sought for the charm of my face.
      Father,
        Mother,
          Sisters all,
God, and myself, I have lost by my fall.
The veriest wretch that goes shivering by
Will take a wide sweep, lest I wander too nigh;

For of all that is on or about me, I know
There is nothing that's pure but the beautiful snow.

How strange it should be that this beautiful snow
Should fall on a sinner with nowhere to go!
How strange it would be, when the night comes again,
If the snow and the ice struck my desperate brain!
      Fainting,
         Freezing,
            Dying alone
Too wicked for prayer, too weak for my moan
To be heard in the crash of the crazy town,
Gone mad in its joy at the snow's coming down
To lie and to die in my terrible woe,
With a bed and a shroud of the beautiful snow.

THE GHASTLY WHITE SNOW

According to an old scrapbook in which I found this, the author
was the editor of the *Belfast Journal*.

Oh, the snow, the, ghastly white snow,
Filling the roads up, four feet or so;
Over the trowsers into tiro boots,
Over the fences, see how it scoots!
      Sifting,
         Drifting,
            More and more,
Business obstructing, confounded bore!

Piling it up where the gals must walk,
Making them wade, with a terrible squawk,
Clinging to gaiters, and garters, and hose
Shivering snow, till they're almost froze.

Oh, the snow, the uncomfortable snow,
Full of the rheumatics, full of all woe,
Whiring about in your troublesome way,
Why not wait till you're wanted—say?

Once we had malls and news that was prime,
Once we had trains that ran on time;
But now the oxen a tri-
Angle is all the travel we spy.
            Jerking,
                Yanking,
                    Squealing along,
Pressing the beautlful flakes of the song.

Too pious to swear, and unable to leave,
How ran we these terrible feelings relieve?
Though blessed with but little perishing wealth
'Twould he worth a dollar, and good for health,
To twist the nose, for a moment or so,
Of that humbug, the author of *Beautiful Snow*.

42.

MAUD MULLER

By John Greenleaf Whittier

Maud Muller on a summer's day
Raked the meadow sweet with hay.

Beneath her torn hat glowed the wealth
Of simple beauty and rustic health.

Singing, she wrought, and her merry glee
The mock-bird echoed from his tree.

But when she glanced to the far-off town,
White from its hill-slope looking down,

The sweet song died, and a vague unrest
And a nameless longing filled her breast,—

A wish that she hardly dared to own,
For something better than she had known.

The judge rode slowly down the lane,
Smoothing his horse's chestnut mane.

He drew his bridle in the shade
Of the apple-trees, to greet the maid,

John Greenleaf Whittier

And asked a draught from the spring that flowed
Through the meadow across the road.

She stooped where the cool spring bubbled up,
And filled for him her small tin cup,

And blushed as she gave it, looking down
On her feet so bare, and her tattered gown.

"Thanks!" said the Judge; "a sweeter draught
From a fairer hand was never quaffed."

He spoke of the grass and flowers and trees,
Of the singing birds and the humming bees;

Then talked of the haying, and wondered whether
The cloud in the west would bring foul weather.

And Maud forgot her brier-torn gown,
And her graceful ankles bare and brown;

And listened, while a pleased surprise
Looked from her long-lashed hazel eyes.

At last, like one who for delay
Seeks a vain excuse, he rode away.

Maud Muller looked and sighed: "Ah me!
That I the judge's bride might be!

"He would dress me up in silks so fine,
And praise and toast me at his wine.

"My father should wear a broadcloth coat:
My brother should sail a painted boat.

"I'd dress my mother so grand and gay,
And the baby should have a new toy each day.

"And I'd feed the hungry and clothe the poor,
And all should bless me who left our door."

The Judge looked back as he climbed the hill,
And saw Maud Muller standing still.

"A form more fair, a face more sweet,
Ne'er hath it been my lot to meet.

"And her modest answer and graceful air
Show her wise and good as she is fair.

"Would she were mine, and I to-day,
Like her, a harvester of hay;

"No doubtful balance of rights and wrongs,
Nor weary lawyers with endless tongues,

"But low of cattle and song of birds,
And health and quiet and loving words."

But he thought of his sisters, proud and cold,
And his mother, vain of her rank and gold.

So, closing his heart, the Judge rode on,
And Maud was left in the field alone.

But the lawyers smiled that afternoon,
When he hummed in court an old love-tune;

And the young girl mused beside the well
Till the rain on the unraked clover fell.

He wedded a wife of richest dower,
Who lived for fashion, as he for power.

Yet oft, in his marble hearth's bright glow,
He watched a picture come and go;

And sweet Maud Muller's hazel eyes
Looked out in their innocent surprise.

Oft, when the wine in his glass was red,
He longed for the wayside well instead;

And closed his eyes on his garnished rooms
To dream of meadows and clover-blooms.

And the proud man sighed, with a secret pain,
"Ah, that I were free again!

"Free as when I rode that day,
Where the barefoot maiden raked her hay."

She wedded a man unlearned and poor,
And many children played round her door.

But care and sorrow, and childbirth pain,
Left their traces on heart and brain.

And oft, when the summer sun shone hot
On the new-mown hay in the meadow lot,

And she heard the little spring brook fall
Over the roadside, through the wall,

In the shade of the apple-tree again
She saw a rider draw his rein;

And, gazing down with timid grace,
She felt his pleased eyes read her face.

Sometimes her narrow kitchen walls
Stretched away into stately halls;

The weary wheel to a spinnet turned,
The tallow candle an astral burned,

And for him who sat by the chimney lug,
Dozing and grumbling o'er pipe and mug,

A manly form at her side she saw,
And joy was duty and love was law.

Then she took up her burden of life again,
Saying only, "It might have been."

Alas for maiden, alas for Judge,
For rich repiner and household drudge!

God pity them both! and pity us all,
Who vainly the dreams of youth recall.

For of all sad words of tongue or pen,
The saddest are these: "It might have been!"

Ah, well! for us all some sweet hope lies
Deeply buried from human eyes;

And, in the hereafter, angels may
Roll the stone from its grave away!

KATE KETCHEM

By Phoebe Gary

Kate Ketchem, on a winter's night,
Went to a party, dressed in white.

Her chignon in a net of gold
Was about as large as they ever sold.

Gayly she went because her "pap"
Was supposed to be a rich old chap.

But when by chance her glances fell
On a friend who lately had married well,

Her spirits sunk, and a vague unrest
And a nameless longing filled her breast

A wish she wouldn't have made known,
To have an establishment of her own.

Torn Fudge came slowly through the throng,
With chestnut hair, worn pretty long.

He saw Kate Ketcham in the crowd,
And, knowing her slightly, stopped and bowed.

Then asked her to give him a single flower,
Saying he'd think it a priceless dower.

Out from those with which she was docked
She took the poorest she could select,

And blushed as she gave it, looking down
To call attention to her gown.

"Thanks," said Fudge, as he thought how dear
Flowers must be at this time of year.

Then several charming remarks he made,
Asked if she sang, or danced, or played;

And being exhausted, inquired whether
She thought it was going to be pleasant weather.

And Kate displayed her jewelry,
And dropped her lashes becomingly;

And listened with no attempt to disguise
The admiration in her eyes.

At last, like one who has nothing to say,
He turned around and walked away.

Kate Ketchum smiled, and said "You bet
I'll catch that Fudge and his money yet.

"He's rich enough to keep me in clothes,
And I think I could manage him if I chose.

"He could aid my father as well as not,
And buy my brother a splendid yacht.

"My mother for money should never fret,
And all that it cried for the baby should get,

"And after that, with what he could spare,
I'd make a show at a charity fair."

Tom Fudge looked back as he crossed the sill.
And saw Kate Ketchern standing still.

"A girl more suited to my mind
It isn't an easy thing to find;

"And everything that she has to wear
Proves her as rich as she is fair.

"Would she were mine, and that I to-day
Had the old man's cash my debts to pay;

"No creditors with a long account,
No tradesmen waiting 'that little amount;'

"But all my scores paid up when due
By a father as rich as any Jew!"

But he thought of her brother, not worth a straw,
And her mother, that would be his, in law;

So, undecided, he walked along,
And Kate was left alone in the throng.

But a lawyer smiled, when he sought by stealth,
To ascertain old Ketchem's wealth;

And as for Kate, she schemed and planned
Till one of the dancers claimed her hand.

He married her for her father's cash—
She married him to cut a dash.

But as to paying his debts, do you know
The father couldn't see it so;

And at hints for help Kate's hazel eyes
Looked out in their innocent surprise.

And when Tom thought of the way he had wed,
He longed for a single life instead,

And closed his eyes in a sulky mood
Regretting the days of his bachelorhood;

And said in a sort of reckless vein,
"I'd like to see her catch me again,

"If I were free as on that night
I saw Kate Ketchem dressed in white!"

She wedded him to be rich and gay;
But husband and children didn't pay.

He wasn't the prize she hoped to draw,
And wouldn't live with his mother-in-law.

And oft when she had to coax and pout
In order to get him to take her out,

She thought how very attentive and bright
He seemed at the party that winter's night.

Of his laugh, as soft as a breeze of the south,
('Twas now on the other side of his mouth:)

How he praised her dress and gems in his talk,
As he took a careful account of stock.

Sometimes she hated the very walls—
Hated her friends, her dinners, and calls:

Till her weak affections, to hatred turned,
Like a dying tallow candle burned.

And for him who sat there, her peace to mar,
Smoking his everlasting segar—

He wasn't the man she thought she saw,
And grief was duty, and hate was law.

So she took up her burden with a groan
Saying only, "I might have known!"

Alas for Kate! and alas for Fudge!
Though I do not owe them any grudge

And alas for any that find to their shame
That two can play at their little game.

For of all hard things to bear and grin,
The hardest is knowing you're taken in.

Ah well! as a general thing we fret
About the one we didn't get;

But I think we needn't make a fuss
If the one we don't want didn't get us.

Maud Muller Mutatur

By Franklin P. Adams,
from **Something Else Again** *(1920)*

Maud Muller, on a summer's day,
Powdered her nose with *Bon Sachet*.

Beneath her lingerie hat appeared
Eyebrows and cheeks that were well veneered.

Singing she rocked on the front piazz,
To the tune of "The Land of the Sky Blue Jazz."

But the song expired oil the summer air,
And she said "This won't get me anywhere."

The judge in his car looked up at her
And signalled "Stop!" to his brave chauffeur.

He smiled a smile that is known as broad,
And he said to Miss Muller, "Hello, how's Maud?"

"What sultry weather this is? Gee whiz!"
Said Maud. Said the judge, "I'll say it is."

"Your coat is heavy. Why don't you shed it?
Have a drink?" said Maud. Said the judge, "You said it."

And Maud, with the joy of bucolic youth,
Blended some gin and some French vermouth.

Maud Muller sighed, as she poured the gin,
"I've got something on Whittier's heroine."

"Thanks," said the judge, "a peppier brew
From a fairer hand was never knew."

And when the judge had had number 7,
Maud seemed an angel direct from Heaven.

And the judge declared, "You're a lovely girl,
An' I'm for you, Maudie, I'll tell the worl'."

And the judge said, "Marry me, Maudie dearie?"
And Maud said yes to the well known query.

And she often thinks, in her rustic way,
As she powders her nose with *Bon Sachet*,

"I never'n the world would 'a got that guy,
If I'd waited till after the First o' July."

And of all glad words of prose or rhyme,
The gladdest are, "Act while there yet is time."

MRS. JUDGE JENKINS

By Bret Harte who described the poem as "being the only
genuine sequel to 'Maud Muller.' "

Maud Muller all that summer day
Raked the meadow sweet with hay;

Yet, looking down the distant lane,
She hoped the Judge would come again.

But when he came, with smile and bow,
Maud only blushed, and stammered, "Ha-ow?"

And spoke of her "pa," and wondered whether
He 'd give consent they should wed together.

Old Muller burst in tears, and then
Begged that the Judge would lend him "ten;"

For trade was dull, and wages low,
And the "craps," this year, were somewhat slow.

And ere the languid summer died,
Sweet Maud became the Judge's bride.

But on the day that they were mated,
Maud's brother Bob was intoxicated;

And Maud's relations, twelve in all,
Were very drunk at the Judge's hall

And when the summer came again,
The young bride bore him babies twain;

And the Judge was blest, but thought it strange
That bearing children made such a change;

For Maud grew broad and red and stout,
And the waist that his arm once clasped about

Was more than he now could span; and he
Sighed as he pondered, ruefully,

How that which in Maud was native grace
In Mrs. Jenkins was out of place;

And thought of the twins, and wished that they
Looked less like the men who raked the hay

On Muller's farm, and dreamed with pain
Of the day he wandered down the lane.

And looking down that dreary track,
He half regretted that he came back;

For, had he waited, he might have wed
Some maiden fair and thoroughbred;

For there be women fair as she,
Whose verbs and nouns do more agree.

Alas for maiden! alas for judge!
And the sentimental,—that's one-half "fudge;"

For Maud soon thought the Judge a bore,
With all his learning and all his lore;

And the Judge would have bartered Maud's fair face
For more refinement and social grace.

If, of all words of tongue and pen,
The saddest are, "It might have been,"

More sad are these we daily see:
"It is, but had n't ought to be."

Maud Muller's Hat

By Anonymous

Maud Muller on a winter's day
Went forth unto the matinee.

With twinkling eyes and rougish smile
She sauntered down the centre aisle.

She sauntered down, and then she sat
Beneath the biggest kind of hat.

I sauntered down the aisle and sat
Behind her continent of hat.

Then, with her hattish hemisphere,
Maud sweetly raked the atmosphere.

I, being five feet three sat there
And gazed upon Maud Muller's hair.

The people all around agreed
The play was very fine indeed.

Maud's hat with sweet excitement swayed
With what the players said and played.

In its wild bobbing here and there
I read joy, pleasure, grief, despair.

When Maud's hat trembled in affright,
I knew the villain was in sight.

And when it wobbled through the air.
I knew the funny man was there.

And when that hat with tremblings bobbed.
Methought the hero-lady sobbed.

At last I 'rose and went my way
From out that weary matinee.

Out to the street I made my way
And paused a bit to sigh and say:

"Of all sad words on earth, I ween,
The saddest are these, 'I might have seen.' "

And I pitied those men, who, like me, sat
Right behind that woman's hat.

THE POLITICAL MAUD

By Eugene Field

I include this parody here only because of the pun at the end of the last line. To understand the political satire you must know that Major-General Benjamin Franklin Buttler, a great Civil War hero, later became a controversial and erratic politician. He was twice defeated as governor of Massachusetts, but eventually was elected on the Democratic ticket. He later sought and lost the Democratic nomination for president of the United States in 1884, the year Field's satire was published. He ran anyway, on the Greenback Party ticket, but was easily defeated.

Gamelial Bradford has a chapter about Butler in his book Damaged Souls *(1923). Field pictures him here as the Maud Muller of Whittier's poem, at first attractive to "Judge Nomination," who reluctantly decides not to vote for "her" because of opposition by his political associates.*

Ben Butler, on a summer's day,
Stood in a convention making hay;
The hay was sweet and the hay was dry,
But it wasn't as cocked as old Ben's eye;
For old Ben saw on a gelding gay
Judge Nomination ride that way.

When the judge saw Ben in the hay at work,
He stopped his horse with a sudden jerk,
And he rolled his eyes on the winsome face
And the buxom form and the air of grace
And the wealth of check and the mesh of hair;
Of sweet Ben Butler a-working there.

"Oh," sighed the judge, "that the fate were mine
To wed with a creature so divine!
With Ben for a mate, my life would seem
Like a poet's song or an artist's dream;
But, when they heard of my marital pick,
How like a steer some folks would kick!"

So, fearful of what his folks might say,
Judge Nomination rode away,
And left Ben Butler standing there
With her wealth of cheek and her mesh of hair;
And of all sad words of tongue and pen
The saddest tire these: "He would n't have Ben."

43.

THE BURIAL OF SIR JOHN MOORE

By Charles Wolfe

Not a drum was heard, not a funeral note,
    As his corse to the ramparts we hurried;
Not a soldier discharged his farewell shot
    O'er the grave where our hero we buried.

We buried him darkly, at dead of night,
    The sods with our bayonets turning,
By the struggling moonbeam's misty light,
    And the lantern dimly burning.

No useless coffin enclosed his breast,
    Not in sheet nor in shroud we wound him;
But he lay like a warrior taking his rest,
    With his martial cloak around him.

Few and short were the prayers we said,
    And we spoke not a word of sorrow;
But we steadfastly gazed on the face that was dead,
    And we bitterly thought of the morrow.

We thought as we hollow'd his narrow bed,
    And smoothed down his lonely pillow,
That the foe and the stranger would tread o'er his head,
    And we far away on the billow!

Lightly they'll talk of the spirit that's gone,
    And o'er his cold ashes upbraid him;
But little he'll reck if they let him sleep on,
    In the grave where a Briton has laid him.

But half of our heavy task was done,
    When the clock struck the hour for retiring,
And we heard the distant and random gun
    That the foe was sullenly firing.

Slowly and sadly we laid him down,
    From the field of his fame fresh and gory;
We carved not a line, and we raised not a stone,
    But we left him alone in his glory.

THE MARRIAGE OF SIR JOHN SMITH

By Phoebe Cary

Not a sigh was heard, nor a funeral tone,
    As the man to his bridal we hurried;
Not a woman discharged her farewell groan,
    On the spot where the fellow was married.

We married him just about eight at night,
    Our faces paler turning,
By the struggling moonbeam's misty light,
    And the gas-lamp's steady burning.

No useless watch-chain covered his vest,
    Nor over-dressed we found him;
But he looked like a gentleman wearing his best,
    With a few of his friends around him.

Few and short were the things we said,
    And we spoke not a word of sorrow,
But we silently gazed on the man that was wed,
    And we bitterly thought of the morrow.

We thought, as we silently stood about,
    With spite and anger dying,
How the merest stranger had cut us out,
    With only half our trying.

Lightly we'll talk of the fellow that's gone,
    And oft for the past upbraid him;
But little he'll reek if we let him live on,
    In the house where his wife conveyed him.

But our heavy task at length was done,
    When the clock struck the hour for retiring;
And we heard the spiteful squib and pun
    The girls were sullenly firing.

Slowly and sadly we turned to go,—
    We had struggled, and we were human;
We shed not a tear, and we spoke not our woe,
    But we left him alone with his woman.

44.

THE OLD OAKEN BUCKET

By Samuel Woodworth

How dear to this heart are the scenes of my childhood,
  When fond recollection presents them to view!
The orchard, the meadow, the deep-tangled wild-wood,
  And every loved spot which my infancy knew!
The wide-spreading pond, and the mill that stood by it,
  The bridge, and the rock where the cataract fell,
The cot of my father, the dairy-house nigh it,
  And e'en the rude bucket that hung in the well—
The old oaken bucket, the iron-bound bucket,
The moss-covered bucket which hung in the well.

That moss-covered vessel I hailed as a treasure,
  For often at noon, when returned from the field,
I found it the source of an exquisite pleasure,
  The purest and sweetest that nature can yield.
How ardent I seized it with hands that were glowing,
  And quick to the white-pebbled bottom it fell;
Then soon, with the emblem of truth overflowing,
  And dripping with coolness, it rose from the well—
The old oaken bucket, the iron-bound bucket,
The moss-covered bucket arose from the well.

How sweet from the green mossy brim to receive it,
  As poised on the curb it inclined to my lips!
Not a full blushing goblet would tempt me to leave it,

211

Though filled with the nectar that Jupitor sips
And now, far removed from the loved habitation,
    The tear of regret will intrusively swell,
As fancy reverts to my father's plantation,
    And sighs for the bucket that hangs in the well—
The old oaken bucket, the iron-bound bucket,
The moss-covered bucket that hangs in the well!

THE OLD HOKUM BUNCOMBE

By Robert E. Sherwood

How dear to my heart are the grand politicians
    Who constantly strive for the popular votes,
Indulging in platitudes, trite repetitions,
    And time-honored bromides surrounded with quotes;
Though equally verbose opponents assail them
    With bitter invective, they never can quell
The force of the buncombe, which never will fail them—
    The old hokum buncombe we all know so well.
The old hokum buncombe, the iron-clad buncombe,
The moss-covered buncombe we all know so well.

They aim to make friends of the laboring classes—
    The trust of the people is sacred with them—
They swear that they're slaves to the will of the masses,
    They hem and they haw, and they haw and they hem;
They rave with a vehemence almost terrific,
    There isn't a doubt which they cannot dispel,
They revel in orgies of hope beatific—
    And serve us the buncombe we all know so well.
The old hokum buncombe, the iron-clad buncombe,
The moss-covered buncombe we all know so well.

Their torrents of words are a sure paregoric
    For all of the ills to which mankind is prey.
They pose as a Hamlet lamenting the Yorick
    Who typifies that which their rivals betray.
They picture perfection in every effusion,
    We gaze at Utopia under their spell,
And though it is only an optic illusion—
    We fall for the buncombe we all know so well.
The old hokum buncombe, the iron-clad buncombe,
The moss-covered buncombe we all love so well.

THE OLD-FASHIONED KITCHEN

By Anonymous

How dear to my heart are the days of my boyhood!
    What chestnuts arise as I call them to mind!
The buttery, the cellar, the big pile of cordwood,
    And the old chopping-block with the kindlings behind.
The wide opened farmyard, the milking stool by it;
    The cow—on her neck hang a discordant bell;
The barn and the cow-house, the chicken-roost nigh it,
    The apple tree—out of its branches I fell,
Near the old-fashioned kitchen, the gable roofed kitchen,
    The old-fashioned kitchen built on in an L.

To hie to that kitchen I deemed it a pleasure,
    For often at noon, when returned from the shop,
I found on the table a half gallon measure
    Filled up to the brim with cold buttermilk pop.
How ardent I seized it, there's really no knowing,
    How quickly I drank it I hardly can tell;
Then soon, with the buttermilk down my chin flowing,
    In a manner on which I dislike now to dwell,
I skipped from the kitchen, that old-fashioned kitchen,
    That old-fashioned kitchen built on in an L.

THAT OLD SMELLY ONION

By Anonymous

How dear to my heart is the loud-smelling onion
    Which restaurant keepers provide at each meal,
The color of silver, the size of a bunion,
    With night-blooming corns wrapped up in each peel.
It stings like a skeeter, it burns like an ember,

And smells like a horse that is silent in death;
And yet with affection and love we remember
   The early spring onion that scented our breath.

The loud-smelling onion, the sweet-perfumed onion,
   The Lubin-like onion that clings to your breath.
You drown it with beefsteak, you boil or you bake it,
   But still it retains its malodorous charm;
And after you've done all you can to forsake it,
   It clings to you fervently, fearing no harm.

Though dangers o'ertake you and troubles awake you,
   At home or abroad, on land or at sea,
The scent of that onion forever will make you
   Desert all your friends or they will shake thee.
That moss-covered onion, that ironbound onion,
   That old "gamey" onion that clings to you still.

THE OLD-FASHIONED HARLOT

By Eugene Field

How dear to my heart is the old-fashioned harlot
When fond recollection presents her to view,
The madam, the whorehouse, and beer by the carlot,
And e'en the delight of the old-fashioned screw.
You may talk as you like of these new innovations
Imported from France and of which I've heard tell,
But give me the natural, carnal sensations
Of the old-fashioned harlot whose surname was Belle.

How dear to my heart was the old-fashioned harlot
As she lay legs outstretched on her sumptuous bed,
While I, an impetuous horny young varlet,
Drove my dink to the hub in her spoiled maidenhead;

With her musk and her smile and her very bad grammar
She had cast over me quite a Paphian spell,
And I dearly delighted to fondle and cram her,
This old-fashioned harlot whose surname was Belle.

How dear to my heart was the old-fashioned harlot
Whose regular price was five dollars a leap,—
I was really quite fond of those women in scarlet
With whom I was wont, on occasion, to sleep;
You may sing as you please of the old-fashioned bucket
That hung or that swung in the moss-girdled well,
But give me a strumpet with leisure to fuck it
Like the old-fashloned harlot whose surname was Belle.

THE OLD RED SUNBONNET

By James Barton Adams

How dear to my heart are the scenes of my childhood
    When fond recollection presents them to view!
The orchard, the meadow, the deep tangled wildwood
    And every fond spot which my infancy knew."
So sang the old poet in rhythmical measure,
    And millions have dreamed of his picture so fair,
But never a word of that one crowning treasure,
    The old red sunbonnet our girls used to wear.

The bells of to-day in their scorn would deride it
    And wonder how maidens could wear such a fright!
But when 'twas protecting a dear head inside it
    To old-fashioned boys 'twas a heavenly sight,
No ornaments decked it, it bore no fine laces,
    No ribbons of bright colored lines did it bear,
But hid in its depths was the sweetest of faces
    That old red sunbonnet our girl used to wear.

When school was dismissed, on her head we would set it
    And tie the long strings in a knot 'neath her chin,
Then claim from her red lips a kiss and would get it,
    For kissing in old days was never a sin.
Then homeward we'd speed where the brooklet was plashing
    Down through the old wood and the meadow so fair,
The skies not more blue than the eyes that were flashing
    Inside that sunbonnet our girl used to wear.

In front of her mirror a proud dame is standing
    Arranging a prize on her head, now so white!
She turns, while her bosom with pride is expanding,
    And asks if it is not a dream of delight!
I speak of the past as I make the inspection,
    Of days when to me she was never more fair,
And tears gem her eyes at the fond recollection
    Of that old sunbonnet she once used to wear.

THE OLD-FASHIONED LATCH-STRING

By Helen Whitney Clarke

The latch-string, how often, when hungry and jaded,
    I grasped it quite carefully, lest it should catch;
For I knew it was tender, its well as much faded,
    So I pulled it down gently to lift up the latch.
The noon meal, when ready, how quickly I seized it—
    A bowlful of mush, with sweet milk brimming o'er;
Not it full blushing goblet could tempt me to leave it,
    When I'd pulled the old latch-string to open the door.

    The old-fashioned latch-string,
    The brown, faded latch-string;
    The long leather latch-string,
    That hung on the door.

And when far away I had strayed from that dwelling,
    Returning, I hailed it with many a shout;
For I knew at a glance—'twas a signal unfailing.
    The folks were at home when the latch string was out!
But they long since have faded, those dreams that I cherished,
    When barefoot I romped on the old puncheon floor;
And the clap-board roofed cabin itself, too, has vanished,
    As well as the latch-string which hung on the door.

    The old-fashioned latch-string,
    The brown, faded latch-string;
    The long leather latch-string,
    That hung on the door.

How dear to my heart is the home of my childhood,
    A lonely log cabin, half-hidden from view;
Where I grew like a weed, springing up in the wildwood,
    And loved the rude home which bad sprung up there, too.
The old lean-to kitchen, the smoke-house beside it;
    The straw stack, with shelter of thatch covered o'er;
The ash-hopper near, where the woodshed could hide it;
    And e'en the rude latch-string which hung on the door.

    The old-fashioned latch-string,
    The brown, faded latch-string;
    The long leather latch-string,
    That hung on the door.

The spring branch still runs at the foot of the meadow,
    Where we cut the tall clover and pastured our flocks;
But the summer time flung o'er my young life a shadow,
    For I hated to cradle and pile up the shocks.
But now, when removed from that loved situation,
    The tears of regret will intrusively pour;
When fancy reverts to that loved habitation,
    And sighs for the latch-string that hung on the door.

The old-fashioned latch-string,
The brown, faded latch-string;
The long leather latch-string,
That hung on the door.

WHEN DAD KICKED THE BUCKET

By J. Howard Flower,
in **Fun from Cover to Cover (1932),**
compiled by Donald and Howard Flower

How dear to my heart was tile home of my childhood,
    Whose family circle my memories view!—
A father, three mothers, and five older brothers,
    And twelve younger girls, and an infant or two.
The wide-spreading swamp and the drain that ran nigh it
    Not far from the well whose sad tale I must tell;
The fate of my father and how he came by it—
    Its cause, the rude bucket that hung in the well.

The old oaken bucket, tile iron-bound bucket,
    The moss-covered bucket that hung in the well.
That moss-covered vessel he hailed as a treasure
    One day when at noon he came in from the field;
He thought 't would relieve in his head the fierce pressure,
    And steadied himself on the curb as he reeled.
How quickly he seized it with hands that were glowing
    And leaned o'er the water that rose from the well—
But alas! 'twas no emblem of truth overflowing,—
    It smote on his nose with a horrible smell.
He swore at that bucket, that slime-covered bucket,—
    That very rude bucket be hung in the well.

How patiently he had left work to receive it!
    Now, poised on the curb, it inclines to his lips.

That growth in his head—how he hopes 't will relieve it,
    Tho not half so good as the whiskey he sips.
But, smelling that stench, with his rage quickly growing,
    He drew back his toe with a curse and a yell,
Made a bound at that bucket and kickt it a-going—
    Lost balance—headfirst, he pitcht into the well.

That rudely-kickt bucket, that iron-bound bucket,
    That poor south-bound bucket shot into the well.
Dad curst as it went, then he followed the bucket—
    Just where he stoppt swearing, O how can I tell—
Which travelled the fastest, or where he o'ertook it?
    —We drew them up sadly and emptied them well.

So now, far removed from that loved habitation,
    My fancy recalls how he damned it to hell—
That water; and weeps at my father's damnation,
    For dad kickt the bucket 'way down in the well.

They got a new bucket and well, when he struck it,
    When dad kicked the bucket that hung in the well.

THE OLD STICKY SCRAPBOOK

By Anonymous

How dear to my heart are the scraps herein pasted,
    As fond recollection presents them to view;
The hours I spent thus were surely not wasted,
    For their pleasures were many and no sorrow they knew.
'Tis my sticky old scrapbook, my paste-covered scrapbook,
    My leather-bound scrapbook that loves me so well.

This child of the scissors and gummy paste pot
    Is endear'd to my heart as its features I view;

'Tis the offspring my patience and pleasure begot,
    And slowly in bigness and beauty it grew.

Gossip, gastronomic; Boniface biographies;
    Stories of clerks with phenomenal cheek;
Tales about countries not found in geographies;
    Tales about the bed-bug, so gentle and meek.

Profound dissertations on all sorts of wonders,
    Both dead and alive, without and with gender;
Grave compositions on comical blunders
    Are neighbors to stories I dare not re-render.

Menus of banquets and Thanksgiving dinners;
    The story of a cockroach embalm'd in a pie;
The incredulous tale of a brace of slick sinners,
    Who slid down a 'scape so conveniently nigh.

And many more subjects, I cannot remember,
    Are discussed in these pages of newspaper scraps.
A great many riddles I cannot remember,
    With elaborate keys and diagram maps,
Are found in this scrap book, this sticky old scrapbook,
    This leather-bound scrapbook that loves me so well.

THE OLD SLOP BUCKET

By J. C. Bayles, from **The Doctor's Window,**
*an 1898 anthology of medical verse
edited by Ina Russelle Warren*

With what anguish of mind I remember my childhood,
    Recalled in the light of a knowledge since gained;
The malarious farm, the wet fungus grown wildwood,
    The chills then contracted that since have remained

The scum-covered duck pond, the pigsty close by it,
    The ditch where the sour smelling house drainage fell;
The damp, shaded dwelling, the foul barnyard nigh it—
    But worse than all else was that terrible well,
And the old oaken bucket, the mold crusted bucket,
    The moss covered bucket that hung in the well.

Just think of it! Moss on the vessel that lifted
    The water I drank in the days called to mind,
Ere I knew what professors and scientists gifted
    In the waters of wells by analysis find;
The rotting wood fiber, the oxide of iron,
    The algae, the frog of unusual size,
The water impure as the verses of Byron,
    Are things I remember with tears in my eyes.

And to tell the sad truth—though I shudder to think it,
    I considered that water uncommonly clear,
And often at noon, when I went there to drink it,
    I enjoyed it as much as I now enjoy beer.
How ardent I seized it with hands that were grimy!
    And quick to the mud covered bottom it fell!
Then reeking with nitrates and nitrites, and slimy
    With matter organic, it rose from the well.

Oh, had I but realized in time to avoid them.
    The dangers that lurked in that pestilent draught,
I'd have tested for organic germs, and destroyed them
    With potassic permanganate ere I had quaffed.
Or, perchance, I'd have boiled it and afterward strained it
    Through filters of charcoal and gravel combined
Or after distilling, condensed and regained it
    In portable form, with its filth left behind.

How little I knew of the dread typhoid fever
    Which lurked in the water I ventured to drink;

But since I've become a devoted believer
  In the teachings of science, I shudder to think.
And now far removed from the scenes I'm describing,
  The story for warning to others I tell,
As memory reverts to my youthful imbibing
  And I gag at the thought of that horrible well,
And the old oaken bucket, the fungus grown bucket—
  In fact, the slop bucket—that hung in the well.

THE POOR LITTLE KITTENS

By Anonymous

An old school speaker, in which I found this, credits it only to the Knickerbocker *magazine.*

How dear to my heart are the scenes of my childhood,
  When fond recollection presents them to view!
The cheese-press, the goose-pond, the pigs in the wild-wood,
  And every old stump that my infancy knew.
The big linkum-basswood, with wide-spreading shadow;
  The horses that grazed where my grandmother fell;
The sheep on the mountain, the calves in the meadow,
  And all the young kittens we drowned in the well.
The meek little kittens, the milk-loving kittens,
  The poor little kittens, we drowned in the well.

I remember with pleasure my grandfather's goggles,
  Which rode so majestic astraddle his nose;
And the harness, oft mended with tow-string and "toggles,"
  That belonged to old Dolly now free from her woes.
And fresh in my heart is the long maple wood-pile,
  Where often I've worked with beetle and wedge,
Striving to whack up enough to last for a good while,
  And grumbling because my old ax had no edge.

And there was the kitchen, and pump that stood nigh it,
    Where we sucked up the drink through a quill in the spout;
And the hooks where we hung tip the pumpkin to dry it;
    And the old cider pitcher, "no doing without:"
The old brown earthen pitcher, the nozzle-cracked pitcher,
    The pain-easing pitcher, "no doing without."

And there was the school-house, away from each dwelling,
    Where school-ma'ams would govern with absolute sway;
Who taught me my 'rithmetic, reading, and spelling,
    And "whaled me like blazes" about every day!
I remember the ladder that swung in the passage,
    Which led to the loft in the peak of the house;
Where my grandmother hung up her "pumpkin and sausage,"
    To keep them away from the rat and the mouse.
But now, far removed from that nook of creation,
    Emotions of grief big as tea-kettles swell,
When Fancy rides back to my old habitation,
    And thinks of the kittens we drowned in the well.
The meek little kittens, the milk-loving kittens,
The poor little kittens, we drowned in the well.

THE OLD-FASHIONED DRESSES

By Carolyn Wells

How dear to this heart are the old-fashioned dresses,
    When fond recollection presents them to view!
In fancy I see the old wardrobes and presses
    Which held the loved gowns that in girlhood I knew.
The wide-spreading mohair, the silk that hung by it;
    The straw-coloured satin with trimmings of brown;
The ruffled foulard, the pink organdy nigh it;
    But, oh! for the pocket that hung in each gown!
        The old-fashioned pocket, the obsolete pocket,
        The praiseworthy pocket that hung in each gown.

That dear roomy pocket I'd hail as a treasure,
  Could I but behold it in gowns of to-day;
I'd find it the source of an exquisite pleasure,
  But all my modistes sternly answer me "Nay!"
'T would be so convenient when going out shopping,
  'T would hold my small purchases coming from town;
And always my purse or my kerchief I'm dropping—
  Oh, me! for the pocket that hung in my gown!
    The old-fashioned pocket, the obsolete pocket,
    The praiseworthy pocket that hung in my gown.

A gown with a pocket! How fondly I'd guard it!
  Each day ere I'd don it, I'd brush it with care;
Not a full Paris costume could make me discard it,
  Though trimmed with the laces an Empress might wear.
But I have no hope, for the fashion is banished;
  The tear of regret will my fond visions drown;
As fancy reverts to the days that have vanished,
  I sigh for the pocket that hung in my gown.
    The old-fashioned pocket, the obsolete pocket,
    The praiseworthy pocket that hung in my gown.

THE HOT ROASTED CHESTNUT

By J. Ed Milliken

How dear to my heart is the hot-chestnut vender,
  Who comes with cold weather, arid goes with the snow!
What finds he to do in the summer, I wonder?
  To the North or the South, which way does he go?
He stands on the corner when chill winds are blowing,
  His fingers alternately burning arid cold,
And stirs tip the chestnuts to keep them from burning—
  I wish he would pick out the bad arid the old!
The sweet toothsome chestnut, the brown-covered chestnut,
  The hot roasted chestnut I remember of old!

The scent of the roasting—what rose can surpass it?
    So fragrant and tempting, the nuts sweet arid brown!
About eleven in the morning I never could pass it,
    With change in my pocket, without coming down.
How eager I seized on the little tin measure,
    And quick in my pockets the contents did pour.
No language could tell all the sweets of the treasure;
    Just try it yourself, and you'll quickly want more.
The tempting ripe chestnut, the soft mealy chestnut,
    The hot misted chestnut we cherished of yore!

The home-made Italians from whom we receive it,
    Some male and some female, my blessings to all!
They may be a nuisance, but I'll not believe it,
    They'd rather roast chestnuts than not work at all.
Although I'm no longer a dear little urchin,
    I cherish the memory of pleasure so sweet;
And while in the season I still will keep munchin'
    The hot roasted chestnut with the sweetest of meat.
The sweet toothsome chestnut, the brown-covered chestnut,
    The hot roasted chestnut that's bought on the street!

THE BOLD SPOKEN LASS WHO HUNG OUT AT THE WELL

By Armand T. Ringer

How dear to this heart are the sins of my childhood,
    When fond recollection presents them to view;
The orchard, the meadow, the deep tangled wildwood,
    And every loved spot that my teen ages knew.
The wide spreading pond, and the mill which stood by it,
    The bridge and the rock where my pantaloons fell,
The cot of my father, the dairy-house nigh it,
    And e'en the young lass who hung out at the well,

That bold spoken lassie, that not-hide-bound lassie,
 That fun loving lass who hung out at the well.

That fun loving lassie I hail as a treasure;
 For often at noon when retired from the field,
I found her the source of an exquisite pleasure,
 The purest and sweetest that nature can yield.
How ardent I seized her with hands that were glowing,
 As quick to her white pimpled bottom they fell;
Then soon with the passion of youth overflowing,
 And dripping with coolness, we rose by the well;
That young lusty lassie, that no-holds-barred lassie,
 That fun loving lassie who rose by the well.

How sweet in that green mossy glen I embraced her,
 As poised on her toes she inclined to my lips!
Not a full blushing goddess could tempt me to leave her,
 No matter how lovely the curves of her hips.
And now, far removed from the loved situation,
 The tears of regret will intrusively swell,
As fancy reverts to my father's plantation
 And sighs for the lass who hung out at the well,
That young bawdy lassie, that firm busted lassie,
 That bold spoken lass who hung out at the well.

45.

MARY'S LITTLE LAMB

By Sarah Hale

Mary had a little lamb,
    Its fleece was white as snow;
And everywhere that Mary went,
    The lamb was sure to go.

He followed her to school one day,
    Which was against the rule;
It made the children laugh and play
    To see a lamb at school.

MARY'S NAUGHTY CAT

By Armand T. Ringer

Mary had a naughty cat.
    Its fur was white as snow;
And everywhere that Mary went,
    The cat was sure to go.

It followed her to school one day,
    Which was against the rule;
Then it approached a stool and left
    A stool beside the stool.

46.

JABBERWOCKY

By Lewis Carroll

'Twas brillig, and the slithy toves
    Did gyre and gimble in the wabe:
All mimsy were the borogoves,
    And the mome raths outgrabe.

"Beware the Jabberwock, my son!
    The jaws that bite, the claws that catch!
Beware the Jubjub bird, and shun
    The frumious Bandersnatch!"

He took his vorpal sword in hand:
    Long time the manxome foe he sought—
So rested he by the Tumtum tree,
    And stood awhile in thought.

And, as in uffish thought he stood,
    The Jabberwock, with eyes of flame,
Came whiffling through the tulgey wood,
    And burbled as it came!

One, two! One, two! And through and through
    The vorpal blade went snicker-snack!
He left it dead, and with its head
    He went galumphing back.

"And hast thou slain the Jabberwock?
    Come to my arms, my beamish boy!
O frabjous day! Callooh! Callay!"
    He chortled in hit joy.

'Twas brillig, and the slithy toves
    Did gyre and gimble in the wabe:
All mimsy were the borogoves,
    And the mome raths outgrabe.

HOLLYWOOD JABBERWOCKY

By Frank Jacobs,
from **Mad for Better or Verse** *(Warner, 1975)*

'Twas Bogart and the Franchot Tones
Did Greer and Garson in the Wayne;
All Muni were the Lewis Stones,
And Rooneyed with Fontaine.

"Beware the deadly Rathbone, son!
Don't Bellamy the Barrymore!
Beware that you the Greenstreet shun,
And likewise Eric Blore!"

He took his Oakie firm in hand,
Long time the Bracken foe to quell;
He stopped to pray at Turhan Bey,
And murmured, "Joan Blondell."

And as he Breened with Jagger drawn,
The deadly Rathbone, eyes Astaire,
Came Rafting through the Oberon
And Harlowed everywhere!

Sabu! Sabu! And Richard Loo!
The Oakie gave a Hardwicke smack!
He seized its Flynn, and with a Quinn,
He went Karloffing back.

"And didst thou Dunne the Rathbone, Ladd?
Come Grable in the Eddy, boy!
O Alice Faye! O Joel McCrea!"
He Cagneyed in his Loy.

'Twas Bogart and the Franchot Tones
Did Greer and Garson in the Wayne;
All Muni were the Lewis Stones,
And Rooneyed with Fontaine.

47.

A VISIT FROM ST. NICHOLAS

By Clement Clarke Moore

'Twas the night before Christmas, when all through the house
Not a creature was stirring, not even a mouse;
The stockings were hung by the chimney with care,
In hopes that St. Nicholas soon would be there;
The children were nestled all snug in their beds,
While visions of sugar-plums danced in their heads;
And Mama in her 'kerchief, and I in my cap,
Had just settled our brains for a long winter's nap;
When out on the lawn there arose such a clatter,
I sprang from the bed to see what was the matter.
Away to the window I flew like a flash,
Tore open the shutters and threw up the sash.
The moon on the breast of the new-fallen snow
Gave the luster of mid-day to objects below,
When, what to my wondering sight should appear
But a miniature sleigh, and eight tiny reindeer,
With a little old driver, so lively and quick,
I knew in a moment it must be St. Nick.
More rapid than eagles his coursers they came,
And he whistled, and shouted, and called them by name:
"Now, *Dasher!* now, *Dancer!* now, *Prancer* and *Vixen!*
On, Comet! on, Cupid! on, Donder and Blitzen!
To the top of the porch! to the top of the wall!
Now dash away! dash away! dash away all!"
As dry leaves that before the wild hurricane fly,

When they meet with an obstacle, mount to the sky,
So up to the house-top the coursers they flew,
With the sleigh full of toys, and St. Nicholas too.
And then, in a twinkling, I heard on the roof
The prancing and pawing of each little hoof—
As I drew in my head and was turning around,
Down the chimney St. Nicholas came with a bound.
He was dressed all in fur from his head to his foot,
And his clothes were all tarnished with ashes and soot;
A bundle of toys he had flung on his back,
And he looked like a peddler just opening his pack.
His eyes—how they twinkled! his dimples how merry!
His cheeks were like roses, his nose like a cherry!
His droll little mouth was drawn up like a bow,
And the beard of his chin was as white as the snow;
The stump of a pipe he held tight in his teeth,
And the smoke it encircled his bead like a wreath;
He had a broad face and a little round belly,
That shook when he laughed, like a bowlful of jelly.
He was chubby and plump, a right jolly old elf,
And I laughed when I saw him, in spite of myself;
A wink of his eye and a twist of his head
Soon gave me to know I had nothing to dread;
He spoke not a word, but went straight to his work,
And filled all the stockings; then turned with a jerk,
And laying his finger aside of his nose,
And giving a nod, up the chimney he rose;
He sprang to his sleigh, to his team gave a whistle,
And away they all flew like the down of a thistle.
But I heard him exclaim, ere he drove out of sight,
"Happy Christmas to all, and to all a good night."

THE NIGHT BEFORE CHRISTMAS, 1999, OR ST. NICHOLAS MEETS THE POPULATION EXPLOSION

By Frank Jacobs, from Mad for Better or Verse (Warner, 1975)

'Twas the night before Christmas, and all through the gloom
Not a creature was stirring; there just wasn't room;
The stockings were hanging in numbers so great,
We feared that the walls would collapse from the weight!
The children like cattle were packed off to bed;
We took a quick count; there were three-hundred head;
Not to mention the grown-ups—those hundreds of dozens
Of uncles and inlaws and twice-removed cousins!
When outside the house there arose such a din!
I wanted to look but the mob held me in;
With pushing and shoving and cursing out loud,
In forty-five minutes I squeezed through the crowd!
Outside on the lawn I could see a fresh snow
Had covered the people asleep down below;
And up in the sky what should strangely appear
But an overweight sleigh pulled by countless reindeer!
They pulled and they tugged and they wheezed as they came,
And the red-suited driver called each one by name:
"Now, *Dasher*! Now, *Dancer*! Now, *Prancer* and *Vixen*!
On, *Comet*! On, *Cupid*! On *Donder* and *Blitzen*!"
"Now, *Melvin*! Now, *Marvin*! Now, *Albert* and *Jasper*!
On, *Sidney*! On, *Seymour*! On *Harvey* and *Casper*!
Now, *Clifford*! Now, *Max*"—but he stopped, far from through:
Our welcoming house-top was coming in view!
Direct to our house-top the reindeer then sped
With the sleigh full of toys and St. Nick at the head;
And then like an earthquake I heard on the roof
The clomping and pounding of each noisy hoof!
Before I could holler a warning of doom,
The whole aggregation fell into the room;

And under a mountain of plaster and brick
Mingled inlaws and reindeer and me and St. Nick;
He panted and sighed like a man who was weary;
His shoulders were stooped
And his outlook was dreary: "I'm way behind schedule,"
He said with a sigh, "And I've been on the road
since the first of July!"
'Twas then that I noticed the great, monstrous sack,
Which he barely could hold on his poor, creaking back,
"Confound it!" he moaned, "Though my bag's full of toys,
I'm engulfed by the birthrate of new girls and boys!"
Then, filling, the stockings, he shook his sad face,
"This job is a killer! I can't take the pace!
This cluttered old world is beyond my control!
There even are millions up at the North Pole!"
"Now I'm late!" he exclaimed, "And I really must hurry!
By now I should be over Joplin, Missouri!"
But he managed to sigh as he drove out of sight,
"Happy Christmas to all, and to all a goodnight!"

48.

THE PURPLE COW

By Gelett Burgess

I never saw a Purple Cow,
  I never hope to see one;
But I can tell you, anyhow,
  I'd rather see than be one.

THE PURPLE SKUNK

By Armand T. Ringer

I never saw a purple skunk.
  I never hope to see one;
But I can tell you what I've thunk,
  I'd rather see than smell one.

APPENDIX.

If Famous Poets Had Different Occupations

By Frank Jacobs, from Mad for Better or Verse
(Warner, 1975)

If RUDYARD KIPLING were a Cookbook Editor

You can talk of beef and spuds,
When you're frocked in fancy duds,
A'sittin' there as cozy as you please;
But when some heathen demon
In your stomach starts a'screamin',
Then you'll sell your bloomin' soul for Buttered Peas.

For it's Peas, Peas, Peas!
They're enough to bring a blighter to his knees!
I'll give up those flying fishes
Long as I've big heaping dishes
Of those succulent, delicious
Buttered Peas!

First you shell 'em to the man,
Then you dump 'em in a pan,
And boil 'em till the bugler calls a halt;
Next remove 'em neat and clean,
While you shout, "God Save the Queen!"
And then serve 'em with some butter and some salt!

For it's Peas, Peas, Peas!
There's no finer food in all the seven seas!

241

It's for you I give my pay for,
Walk the road to Mandalay for;
To the God above I pray for
Buttered Peas!

If WALT WHITMAN were a Greeting Card Writer

O Valentine! My Valentine!
Your face is everywhere;
I see it in the dead leaves;
I see it in the toadstools in the wood;
I see it in the lake scum and the swamp moss;
But I do not see it in the peat bogs;
O Valentine!
You are the bullfrog croaking and the jackal
    howling and the buzzard screaming,
And occasionally the gopher thinking;
My heart is nature's toothpaste tube, and
    you are the force eternal that squeezes
    out the final, itsy-bitsy sweetness;
O me!
O you!
O me! O you!
O you! O me!
O us!
O Valentine!

If ROBERT W. SERVICE wrote the Weather Report

A mass of cool air is churning it up
    Down the-whole Atlantic coast,
And out in the West it's so dog-dirty hot
    That it's making a rattlesnake roast;
In Ohio some snow is beginning to blow
    And they're due for a blizzard or two;
And up in the skies, folks are peeling their eyes
    For the Hurricane known as Sue!

In North Idaho nights are 50 below
    From a cold front up Canada way;
And that low-pressure mass that had started to pass
    Just keeps hanging around day to day;
They're choking from dust from a high-pressure gust
    That keeps blowing from Texas right through,
And from here to Moline folks are looking real keen
    For that Hurricane known as Sue!

They're flooded from rains on the Great Western Plains,
    And from Michigan on to the East,
They're starting to freeze from a cold, icy breeze
    That ain't fit for a man or a beast;
You all wonder, I guess, from this weatherman's mess,
    If the forecast's for rain or for shine—
If everything fails, flip a coin heads or tails,
    'Cause your guess is no better than mine!

If CARL SANDBURG were a Baseball Writer

Play Butcher of the League,
Goof Maker, Dropper of Flies,
Boater of Grounders and the Nation's Ball-Fumbler;
Hitless, runless, winless,
Team of the Big Blunders:
They tell me you are losers, and I believe them, for
    I have seen your hitters be thrown out trying to
    stretch a bunt into a triple.
And they tell me you are deficient, and I answer: Yes,
    it is true I have seen your clean-up man go 0-for-5,
    get benched, then return to go 0-for-5 again.
And they tell me you are hopeless, and my reply is:
    On the faces of your rookies I have seen the marks
    of grief and despair.
And having answered I ask myself: How is it possible
    that nearly two million fans buy tickets every year

to see the Play Butcher of the League, Goof Maker,
Dropper of Flies, Booter of Grounders, and
Ball-Fumbler to the Nation?

If EUGENE FIELD Sold Fresh Fish

Herring, Salmon, and Cod are out,
    So better take something else—
Why not Flounder or Rainbow Trout?
    Or maybe a dozen Smelts?
Mackerel's tasty and, if you wish,
    My Haddock I'll guarantee;
I'll sell you almost any fish
    That comes from the beautiful sea;
    But kindly don't be asking me
        For Herring,
        Salmon,
        Or Cod!

I've Whitefish and Bluefish, Swordfish and Pike;
    My Fluke is a steal for the price;
Red Snapper's delicious, or maybe you'd like
    A Bass that's especially nice;
Sturgeon is making an elegant dish;
    My mullets are fine as can be;
I'll part with almost any fish
    That comes from the beautiful sea;
    But kindly don't be asking me
        For Herring,
        Salmon,
        Or Cod!

I've Catfish and Dogfish, Minnows and Eels;
    Perchance you are craving some Squid?
A Marlin will give your a dozen good meals
    I'll throw in a pot and a lid;

As soon as you're telling me what you wish
    I'll wrap it in paper for free;
I'll let you have most any fish
    That comes from the beautiful sea;
    But kindly don't be asking me
        For Herring,
        Salmon,
        Or Cod!

If WILLIAM BLAKE Were a TV Critic

Buckley! Buckley, on my tube,
Making me feel like a boob;
Would that I could comprehend
Thy gift of gab that does not end.

Buckley! Buckley, spouting on,
Like a human lexicon;
Must thy be so dull and deep
That thy viewers fall asleep?

Buckley! Buckley, I implore,
Bore me with thy words no more—
Else I'll give my set a click
And watch instead a Bogart flick.